Washington's Audacious State Capitol and Its Builders

State Capitol group from Capitol Lake

Washington's Audacious State Capitol and Its Builders

NORMAN J. JOHNSTON

University of Washington Press   *Seattle and London*

This book is published by the University of Washington Press as part of its celebration of the Washington Centennial.

This work was published with the assistance of grants from the American Institute of Architects Foundation and generous contributions from Mr. Leavitt S. White and an anonymous donor.

Library of Congress Cataloging-in-Publication Data

Johnston, Norman J.
  Washington's audacious state capitol and its builders.
  Bibliography: p.
  Includes index.
  1. Washington State Capitol (Olympia, Wash.)
2. Public buildings—Washington (State)—Olympia.
3. Olympia (Wash.)—Buildings, structures, etc.
I. Title.
NA4227.04J64 1987   725′.11′0979779   86-28287
ISBN 0-295-96467-7

To Dad

1886–1969

Contents

State Capitol group from Capitol Lake

Preface

Mention Washington's state Capitol and you will inevitably be understood to mean that proud domed presence on the heights facing north over Olympia and lower Puget Sound. Yet technically Washington has no single capitol building but rather a capitol *group,* of which the dominant unit is the domed Legislative Building—which also dominates this history. For this book is essentially the story of that building, not just as an architectural achievement but as evidence of the economic, political, and especially the human circumstances that shaped it.

The Legislative Building has already had its golden anniversary of service to the state and approaches its diamond jubilee in 1988, just as the state approaches its centennial of statehood the following year. It was completed in 1928, close to the end of a splendid era in the history of monumental architecture, and was almost the last example of that era's unique American contribution: the state capitol. Conceived in the imperial classical manner of what has been called the "American Renaissance" and sharing in the last expression of the City Beautiful Movement, only one state capitol* responding to the same inspiration was to be built after Olympia's. Other capitols used different design approaches, more in harmony with the realities of the post-depression years and the changing intellectual and artistic ambitions of their times.

The West Virginia Capitol (1930–32) by Cass Gilbert.

Nevertheless, there is gradually re-emerging an appreciation, perhaps grudging, of this episode in grand American civic art. A recent show at the Museum of Modern Art and a rash of publications dealing with the Beaux Arts period of the nineteenth and early twentieth centuries in architecture have inspired more sympathetic looks at some of the products of that period. Their grandeur, the richness of their detail, their evocative skylines and dramatic interior spaces are again winning appreciation for their power and for the creative imaginations from which they sprang.

The Capitol group in Olympia shares in this reevaluation and renewed appreciation. Though its planning concept was the product of the headier years of the City Beautiful Movement, intervening events postponed construction of the dominant partner of the group, the Legislative Building. This provided the architects with an additional decade to reflect and grow professionally, years that they used well, judging from the contrasts between their original proposals and what was finally built. An artistic and a technical triumph, their design has worn well and will continue to do so.

This is especially true of the dome. While uncertainly claimed over the years by state publicity to be the fourth highest in the world (after St. Peter's in Rome, St. Paul's in London, and our nation's capitol), nevertheless its height of 278 feet places it in exalted company among the great examples of the idiom. Furthermore, unlike some of its peers, with their metal framing and outer shells (e.g., the National Capitol in Washington, D.C.), this dome is a self-supporting masonry construction, one of the last of that venerable lineage of monumental dimensions. But more important than its measurements is the dome's visual design, the most tangible evidence of the benefits of those extra ten years, during which the architects discovered more enduring alternatives.

My father was the resident supervisor of the construction of our Capitol. As a boy, in the days when construction safety standards and hard-hat areas were as yet unknown, I was given a remarkably free rein to wander about the building during its construction, and on the site or at home to listen in on some of the related technical conversations and political gossip that marked those years. As was the case with other buildings of the same genre, state politics and personal ambitions were never very far removed from the processes that gradually led to the building's completion.

For years my father's files were in the basement of our family home in Olympia until they were finally turned over to the Archives Division of Suzzallo Library at the University of Washington to become an important documentary resource for historians' understanding of the building. Additions were made to those documents in 1975 as the result of my correspondence and subsequent visits with the son of Harry K. White, one of the partners of the project architects, Wilder and White of New York City. Leavitt S. White turned over to me all of what he still had of his father's professional records, which I in turn donated to Suzzallo. He also told me that before learning of my interest in the building and Wilder and White's role in it, he had donated a larger collection of his father's records to the University of Oregon Library at its request. These included account books, miscellaneous presentation and contract drawings, and some documents and photographs related to the Capitol (though the original tracings, and most of the Capitol project office records, have disappeared). Fortunately, the Oregon Library acknowledged that the relevance of these materials to its collection was remote and agreed to transfer them to the University of Washington. Thus, the Suzzallo Library now holds a considerable set of the extant documents related to Olympia's State Capitol group, but not the entirety. In Olympia is the collection at the Washington State Archives, and further photographic records are there with the Department of General Administration and among the State Capitol Museum holdings. I consulted all of these in assembling the resources for this study. Thanks also to my friend Bob Anderson for his field discoveries about Wilder's last days in New York State.

The staffs of the Archives, the Museum, and the Department of General Administration have been consistently helpful, as has been the staff of the Suzzallo Library. I especially wish to note the enthusiasm and interest shown by Dennis A. Andersen, formerly of the Suzzallo Library's Special Collections Division. Key evidence for the unfolding of the story of the 1893 competition was revealed by his watchful eye. Sid Snyder, the secretary of the Washington State Senate, and Dean Foster and Vito Chiechi, both chief clerks of the House of Representatives at the time of this writing, gave me authorizations for easy access to people and places in the Capitol campus important to my research. In practice, this often meant turning to the Senate facilities planner, Dee R. Hooper, whose own enthusiasm for the Legislative Building has contributed to the care and detail of its current rehabilitation program. Francis Brown, then head of the Legislative Building's guide service, was ever available for arranging personal visits to the building or for offering leads to other likely informants. The late G. Noyes Talcott of the pioneer Olympia family kindly reminisced with me about one of the partners of the firm, Walter R. Wilder, and the years the architect was in Olympia in connection with Wilder and White's Capitol campus work.

Specific mention is also deserved for the continuing interest and contributions to this history by Robert F. Arndt, Director of Facilities Planning for the Department of General Administration. His photographs and his discovery of additional correspondence relating particularly to early campus site development have been especially valuable.

Early financial boosts for the publication of the manuscript came with two grants from the College of Fellows Fund of the American Institute of Architects in Washington, D.C.—especially appreciated at a time when local interest seemed so elusive.

Foremost has been the cooperation and assistance generously and graciously provided me by Leav White. His interest in my research, material backing, and hospitality during my visits with him in Delaware and here in Seattle have established an enduring friendship, echoing that which earlier grew between his father and mine.

It has been a pleasure to work again with the University of Washington Press; its Editor-in-Chief Naomi Pascal, who gave the manuscript her crucial support; my editors Veronica Seyd and Marian Bock, quick to discover ambiguities and make needed corrections; and designer Audrey Meyer, under whose deft hand the book took the form in which it has come to its readers. And finally, my appreciation to the Center for Design and Planning of my own college for arranging the transposing of the manuscript to the word processor, a key present-day step toward publication.

Norman J. Johnston

Seattle, Washington

Detail, 1879 bird's eye view of Olympia.
The Territorial Capitol is at the far left, center.

Introduction

State capitols and skyscrapers have been recognized as America's unique contribution to the world's monumental architecture,[1] and the Washington State Capitol group in Olympia provides an added dimension. For instead of construction of a single building to reflect suitably the needs and aspirations of state government, a plan was chosen for a *group* of buildings. In its time, this century hardly a decade old, it was an unprecedented idea in our national experience, especially audacious for a state with scarcely over 800,000 inhabitants.*

The present-day splendor of Olympia is the result of events that took place over a long period but were all played out in the same theater, a site on heights looking north over the most southerly arm of Puget Sound. It was in Olympia that the first territorial legislature met in 1854, thereby acknowledging the recently founded village's status as port of entry for Puget Sound and the area's relatively large population in the territory (996 residents, exceeded only by Clark County's 1,134).[2]

Olympia had captured a prize when it attracted the territorial legislature. In the nineteenth and early twentieth centuries, speculators in new towns in the developing western regions placed high value on such institutions as capitols, county courthouses, colleges, and penitentiaries, as signs of public commitment to the town's stability and future prosperity. Although Olympia was intermittently forced through the years to defend its status as capital— even as late as 1958—it has remained the capital, first of the territory, now of the state.

The founder of Olympia, Edmund Sylvester, offered twelve acres of land as a site for the Capitol. Although rather remote from the center of town, its timbered heights offered views opening north to Olympia, Puget Sound (Budd Inlet), and the distant Olympics. Below the bluffs on two sides were tidelands, handsome enough when the tide was in, less so when it was out. The acceptance of the Sylvester offer by the legislature in 1855 was an important victory for those who later sought to secure Olympia's status as state capital.

The earliest sessions of the legislature had been held in rented quarters downtown, but in 1856 the legislature moved to its own modest two-story wood-frame building for which Congress had appropriated $5,000. It was located on the Sylvester site in about the same place as today's Legislative Building. Although conceived as a temporary arrangement until more permanent construction could be managed, it served the capital needs of first the territory and then the state until 1903. The permanence of impermanent construction is remarkably common in institutional history.

Circumstances encouraging more monumental ambitions came with statehood. Congress had passed enabling legislation which in 1889 admitted Washington to the Union as the forty-second state. But the federal government had also taken another crucial step, in effect making a gift to the state of its capitol campus construction. In his proclamation of congressional approval of the state's new constitution, President Harrison announced the donation of 132,000 acres of land, to be chosen from any

*In 1911, Washington had a population of 800,132, ranking twenty-sixth among the then forty-six states of the union.

The Territorial Legislative Hall,
in use as the state capitol until 1903

unappropriated federal lands within the state, the income from which was to be used solely for the "erection of buildings at the state capital."[3] These capitol lands, most of them located in the valuable timber areas west of the Cascades, constituted a reserve of wealth from which the state was authorized to draw in building its new capitol and from which it continues to draw to the present day.

There was another, perhaps unanticipated, benefit from this federal generosity. It relieved much of the legislative and public nervousness and the political pressures usually associated with the funding of such ambitious projects as a new capitol. Any general fund expenditures and bonding obligations for the capitol could be made with the anticipation that repayment would come from the selling of capitol lands timber. Thus, on completion of the present Legislative Building the secretary of the State Capitol Committee was able to note that "the present structures will not cost the taxpayers one cent."[4]

Perhaps the availability of income from the timber lands explains the comparatively apolitical nature of much of the Capitol's history. For in contrast to the abrasiveness and trauma that marked the efforts of many states in their pursuit of similar objectives, Washington's construction of its Capitol was relatively serene, not only in the years that are the central focus of this book but in the years that followed.

Washington was granted statehood in 1889, but the first state legislature, pressed by more immediate concerns, did not turn to the question of a new capitol until four years later, when it approved "An Act to provide for the location and erection of a capitol building and providing an appropriation thereto of $500,000." Approved also was the creation of a State Capitol Commission charged with bringing about the construction of a permanent state capitol scaled to state needs and ambitions. Washington was now prepared financially and administratively to undertake this solemn and symbolic task.

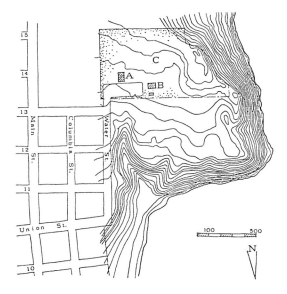

Sylvester donation and Territorial Capitol
site, topography, and location plan, 1856
A Territorial Capitol
B Unidentified accessory buildings
C Original Sylvester donation

I. The Competition of 1893

At its first meeting on July 26, 1893, the new five-member State Capitol Commission organized itself by selecting Governor John H. McGraw as its chairman. It then began its plans for announcing a nationwide competition to select an architect and develop a program of building needs. This included arrangements for surveying the Capitol site so that accurate topographic information could be provided to the competing architects when the program was issued.[1]

The commission moved quickly, for the next day its minutes recorded instructions to architects:

Plans and designs for a State Capitol Building will be received until 2 pm on the 14th Day of December, 1893, at the office of the State Capitol Commission in the City of Olympia, State of Washington.

Said building is to be fire-proof and to be built of stone, brick, iron and steel as far as practicable, and to be equipped with the most approved methods of heating, draining, and ventilating. The entire cost of the building complete, including all fixtures and appliances, ready for occupancy, shall not exceed the sum of One million dollars.[2]

Carl August Darmer capitol design proposal

Each architect was to submit "four elevations, plans of each story, one section and one perspective drawing. These and no others will be considered."[3] The announcement further established (what was characteristic of the times) that all branches of government would be accommodated in a single building. The final "General Instructions to Architects" were approved by the commission on August 24 with no significant departure from their original form.[4] By the competition's December closing date the commission had received 188 submissions, a remarkabe show of interest by the design fraternity of the day. (The competition of 1911 for the present Legislative Building's architect had only thirty entries.)

The *Washington Standard,* an Olympia weekly that followed the competition quite closely, reported on February 9 that the commission was proceeding with the assistance of an imported "expert," Professor William H. Ware of the Department of Architecture at Columbia College (now Columbia University). In choosing Ware the commission sought the advice of the preeminent architectural academician of the day. He had been a founding member (in 1868) of the Massachusetts Institute of Technology's Department of Architecture, and in 1881 he played a similar role in establishing an architectural program at Columbia and then accepted that college's invitation to join its faculty.[5]

Little remains today to indicate the range of proposals forwarded to the commission, since all the drawings except those of the first prize winner appear to have been returned to their authors or otherwise disposed of. Chance, however, has turned up three of these other drawings, whose characteristics are interesting evidence of the state of the design profession at that time.

The submission of Carl August Darmer, a Prussian-born and European-trained architect from Tacoma, is the most heavy-handed and economically unrealistic, even considering the value of one million dollars in those days. With overtones of the ponderousness of Berlin's Reichstag Building of the 1880s, Darmer's dome might have been adequate for a much smaller building but is clearly not up to the task of monumentally crowning this one.

John Parkinson capitol design proposal

William Cowe and George F. Harvey capitol design proposal

John Parkinson, of Seattle but originally from England via Canada, also reflected his national roots in his proposal. The body of his building is well proportioned and scholarly, quite in the manner of the government architecture of London, a setting in which it would have been comfortable. But, again, his uncertainty in handling the dome, with its uncontrolled multiplicity of classical design themes, entirely negates the building's more satisfying features.

By rejecting the third of the trio, the commission may unknowingly have avoided an embarrassment. For what the nonarchitects William Cowe and George F. Harvey of Denver had forwarded was a blatantly faithful copy of the 1886 Colorado Capitol, slightly modified for the Olympia competition, and not necessarily for the better. Unfortunately, Cowe and Harvey made no effort to restudy their model's weakest feature, its dome; they left it almost entirely unaltered in their entry drawings.

Colorado State Capitol, Denver

Professor Ware's first-place selection was the work of a young architect who would soon establish a national reputation, Ernest Flagg of New York City. His participation in the Olympia competition came in the earliest years of his career, when his reputation was still to be established. Nevertheless, for Ware the Flagg proposal "inspired confidence in its author, as does the paper which accompanies the drawings, and it would seem as if the commission could hardly make a mistake if they intrusted the work to his hands."[6]

Flagg's design was for a compact structure with a rusticated ground floor, two main floors, and an attic. It had a certain contemporary "Gilded Age" floridness to it, especially in the dome, which was marred by too many structural and decorative ideas crowded around the drum and layered over the outer shell. He also had his capitol face south, turning its back on the dramatic vista toward town and sound.

But Ware appreciated the design's realistic cost estimates, the "elegant and scholarly" handling of the plan, and its elevations, which were individualistic "without in any way being queer or fantastic." The commission agreed, and on April 26, 1894, awarded its first prize to the Ernest Flagg entry.[7]

Flagg arrived in May to begin translating his competition proposals into specific documents for proceeding with construction. On July 6 the commission approved his new plans, declared itself satisfied that the building costs would fit the authorized budget, and formally appointed him as architect, setting his fee at five percent of actual construction costs.[8]

First prize, Washington State Capitol Building Competition, 1893, Ernest Flagg, architect

Following initial excavation, a Spokane firm carried out the construction of foundations and basement, consisting of brick walls and exterior facing of gray Tenino stone. Total cost of this first phase was about $90,000.[9] But this phase was never to be succeeded by others, for the building was victimized by both economics and politics. The 1895 legislature had authorized a further appropriation of $930,000 for Flagg's building, but the financial depression of the time discouraged sale of the warrants. In 1897 a new appropriation was passed by the legislature, this time for only $500,000.

In the meantime, there had been a change of administration. Governor McGraw, a Republican, and commission chairman at the time of the Flagg appointment, had been succeeded by Governor John R. Rogers, a Democrat from Puyallup, who was thought to favor Tacoma as the state capital rather than Olympia. Delaying the construction of a permanent building to house state functions would, of course, leave the capital city question open to further debate. The new governor could cite the inauspicious economic climate as a reason for postponing construction of the capitol, "a luxury which the people of Washington can at the present time do without."[10] Thus expressing his views on the matter, Governor Rogers vetoed this latest appropriation.

The new governor preferred to have the state purchase the overbuilt Thurston County Courthouse (1892) in downtown Olympia, and in 1901 the legislature gave him the money to make the move. The legislature occupied the building in 1905, and there it remained for the next twenty-two years.[11] Also remaining for some thirty years were the yawning spaces and foundation work of the Flagg building, until they were finally put out of their misery by absorption into the construction of the present Legislative Building.*

*More extensive coverage of the 1893 competition can be found in the author's "A Capitol in Search of an Architect," Pacific Northwest Quarterly 73, no. 1 (January 1982), pp. 2–9.

Old State Capitol, formerly the Thurston County Courthouse (1892), showing new east wing being added to accommodate the legislature and additional state offices

II. The Competition of 1911

By the time Washington returned to efforts toward housing its legislature in a manner befitting state aspirations and ambitions, a considerable change had been worked in the American experience and the environmental devices for expressing it. The public client and its architects had embraced new design goals, in large part influenced by the example set by the Columbian Exposition held in Chicago in 1893, the year of the first Washington competition. The Exposition's "Great White City," an architectural evocation of Imperial Rome, had had the added impact of coordinating the various elements composing the environment into a unified whole. For the American observer it was an unprecedented experience in unity and coordination of architecture, building heights, spatial relationships, and landscape. The scale was big, the details rich, and the sense of national wealth and power pervasive.

The Exposition had also appeared at a time of emerging professional prominence of American architects trained in the French École des Beaux Arts methods of architectural design and planning or familiar with the work of its chief practitioners such as Richard Morris Hunt, George B. Post, Cass Gilbert, Carrère and Hastings, and, most particularly, the firm of McKim, Mead and White. The eclecticism of their architectural taste, the skill with which they worked in large monumental scale, the increasing ease with which they translated classical Roman models for contemporary purposes, and the application of lessons learned, not only brought unprecedented design standards and cohesiveness to American architectural practice but also served to establish new goals for the design of cities as well.

These developments came, too, at a time in American history when the country was beginning to see itself in different ways. The swift victory in the Spanish American War, our sudden acquisition of an overseas empire, and the enormous economic power that the nation had assembled encouraged a

View of Columbian Exposition, Chicago, 1893

Howells* and Stokes. Yet the major architects of the era, some of whom were or had recently been working in other states on similar projects, were missing: Cass Gilbert (Minnesota Capitol), McKim, Mead and White (Rhode Island Capitol), George Post (Wisconsin Capitol), and Arthur Brown, Jr. (San Francisco City Hall). One thinks also of other missing practitioners of the American Renaissance, such as John M. Carrère and Thomas Hastings, John Russell Pope, Daniel Burnham, and Arnold W. Brunner. All were doing work on a scale comparable to that represented by the 1911 competition and might have been expected to be attracted to it.

As things turned out, the 1911 competition was a somewhat local affair. Eighteen entries—over half—were from firms listing Washington addresses; thirteen of those were from Seattle. (In some cases, submittals involved collaborative arrangements, temporary associations by which an out-of-state firm shared the benefits of both out-of-state and in-state identity; in such cases addresses are credited to both states involved, thus accounting for a total greater than thirty.) Other areas were represented by two entries from Oregon, four from California, five from New York, and one each from Duluth, St. Louis, and Denver.[10]

On July 31 the jury of three architects, Bebb, Cutter, and Faville, met to begin the judging process. The thirty submittals were opened before them and stamped with a number which was to be their only identification until after the winning entry had been selected. The judging occupied the following three days. On August 3 the jury reached its conclusions and gave its report to the assembled State Capitol Commission:

The decision of the jury was unanimous and was concurred in unanimously by a full meeting of the State Capitol Commission. When the envelope having the number noted on the drawings was opened by the Governor in presence of the Judges of the Supreme Court, the State Capitol Commission and the Jury of Architects it was found that Messrs. Wilder and White, Architects of New York City had won the competition.[11]

Not only had this firm won the Temple of Justice competition but the group plan award was theirs as well. Two relatively young architects (both in their mid-thirties) out of distant New York City, with only a modest local practice there and no known reputation in Washington, had swept the field.†

*John Mead Howells, in partnership with Raymond M. Hood, won the 1922 Chicago Tribune Competition with an entry for a steel-frame tower in French Gothic sheathing.

†The runners-up were Howells and Stokes, New York, second prize; David J. Myers, Seattle, third prize; Wilcox and Sayward, Seattle, fourth prize; and Ernest Flagg, New York, fifth prize. Honorable mentions were Gilbert Lounsburgh, San Francisco; Milton Lichtenstein, San Francisco; W. Marbury Somervelle, Seattle; William Macomber, Seattle; and J. A. Longe and Lawrence Ewald, St. Louis. The Olmsted brothers of Brookline, Massachusetts, were employed by the commission as landscape architects (The American Architect, vol. C, no. 186 [September 13, 1911], p. 108).

III. The Wilder and White Entry

Who were these conquerors from out of the east and what had they devised to manage their coup? Wilder and White had been partners for five years when they entered Washington's capitol competition. Walter Robb Wilder, the older of the two, was from Kansas but had an eastern education: Phillips Academy, Andover, and architecture at Cornell. He earned his Bachelor of Science in Architecture in 1896 and, degree in hand, was hired in April 1897 by the premier training office for young architects at the turn of the century, McKim, Mead and White. Except for two years of European travel and study in 1900–1902, he continued with the firm until 1906. McKim, Mead and White was at the height of its professional reputation, nationally in demand for the imperial manner in which its designs satisfied the business, institutional, and personal aspirations of its clients. A finishing school for architects, its alumni spread the firm's American Renaissance design specialization from coast to coast.*

It was there that Wilder met another young draftsman, just graduated in 1899 from the Massachusetts Institute of Technology's Department of Architecture, who had been with the firm since August of that year. Two years younger than Wilder, Harry Keith White† was a Vermont-born easterner living in New York City. The two men worked at McKim, Mead and White for a number of years handling a variety of responsibilities for the office's large-scale residential projects and some of its smaller institutional work.

In 1906 the office was thrown into confusion by the shooting death of Stanford White, and perhaps this precipitated thoughts of change, for first Wilder in February 1906 and then White in April 1907 left the firm, and together they formed their own partnership for the practice of architecture. They worked out of an office in downtown New York, although neither man would be living in the city. Wilder and his wife lived to the north in Bronxville, and White was more and more drawn southwest to Plainfield, New Jersey, where his sister was teaching. In due course he married into one of the town's substantial families (its mayor's) and Plainfield became his home for the rest of his life.

The two men maintained a stable professional relationship, though their physically separated domestic arrangements discouraged social contact. Wilder may have been more of the designer, White filling a managerial and production role. But decisions were made in easy give-and-take discussions between them; their association was a close one over the years of their partnership. Both did contact work in search of clients; in this White may have been the more successful, as many of their larger commissions were for schools and institutions in the Plainfield area.[1]

The architectural solutions the partners offered their clients were unpretentiously traditional and classical, reflecting both their own design loyalties and the training and tempo of their times. None of their commissions offered them opportunities for work of a monumental scale, either in the early years of the partnership or later—with the single exception of Olympia's Capitol group.

*Its alumni included such figures as Cass Gilbert, John M. Carrère, Thomas Hastings, William E. Whilden, A. D. F. Hamlin, Henry Bacon, Philip Sawyer, and Egerton Swartwout (*The Brooklyn Museum*, The American Renaissance, 1876–1917, p. 79).*

†No relation to the Stanford White of his employers' firm.

Walter Robb Wilder

The State Capitol Commission's announcement of its competition had been issued to the architectural community in May 1911, and Wilder and White decided to enter. They were primed for the effort, having recently entered another such competition for an important New York public building; although they failed to place in it, the experience had whetted their skills. The Washington competition was therefore timely.

Work on their competition solution and presentation drawings had all the last-minute tensions associated with traditional Beaux Arts methods of working. In an undated letter (mailed July 24, 1911, but written earlier) White reported to his fiancée, Miss Elizabeth Fitz Randolph, on the partners' flurry of activity:

Your letter came yesterday morning when we were on the last lap of the competition. We had thought we could call it done but we found that that was not possible and as long as the Express Co were open to receiving packages until six that we might as well take the extra time for a few finishing touches. As it was, it was but three minutes of six when the drawings were laid on the counter and we were entitled to rest, a shave and hair cut some of which I've had and the rest of which I'm getting gradually. I stayed in New York Thursday and Friday nights and by working until one we were able to finish without undue strain. I think it was our best effort so far and consequently am pleased with the result.

The drawings all looked well and I feel that we had a most logical solution. Those who saw our scheme, other than ourselves, shared this opinion. But it is a long chance with 60 others.

Harry Keith White

As the competition required, their presentation was in two parts, a total of six sheets of drawings.* The group plan dealt with the total campus site, which at that time was closed on the east by Water Street and on the south by a westerly extension of Fifteenth Street. The other perimeters were the bluffs above the tidelands of Budd Inlet. The Flagg foundations, of course, determined the location of the Legislative Building. A north-south axis running centrally through the campus was marked to its south by a semicircular memorial plaza between two flanking office buildings at angles to it, and to the north through the symmetrically placed Temple of Justice laid across it and on down broad monumental stairs and successive landings to a roundabout and connecting shoreline boulevard. In the angle of the bluffs between these stairs and Water Street, the architects indicated an outdoor amphitheater for assemblies on great public occasions, as called for in the competition program. The intersection of the north-south axis and the axis extending east-west through Thirteenth Street occurred at the center of the great oval plaza which both the Legislative Building and the Temple of Justice paralleled. This secondary axis also marked the east approach to the campus. At its west end at another roundpoint it turned northwest, closed by the entrance facade of the relocated Governor's Mansion. Balancing the plan were two additional office buildings on either side of the Legislative Building.

*Neither Wilder and White's drawings nor those of the other competitors remain. However, The American Architect for September 13, 1911, published those submitted by Wilder and White as well as the second prize design from the New York firm of Howells and Stokes. There was more generous local coverage; both The Pacific Coast Architect (September 1911) and the Pacific Builder and Engineer (October 14, 1911) included reproductions of drawings from eight of the prize-winning and honorable mention entries. As for Wilder and White's original construction drawings, they too have been lost. When the firm was dissolved in 1930, in the division of its records those associated with the firm's work in Olympia went to Wilder. What became of them after his death is unknown; they were presumably destroyed in the general disposition of his belongings. Therefore, prints alone make up the bulk of documentary evidence of the partners' Olympia designs and their development. For the competition, the most accessible are those included in The American Architect for September 13, 1911, which also included prints of the second prize design.

These losses, and the loss of records from the partners' New York office, have complicated the task of tracing the evolution of the designs for the group plan and its units. Almost any interpretation of influences, models, etc., must be substantially inferential.

Accepted group plan design, Wilder and White, architects

The elevation reaffirmed the balanced order of the group plan. All buildings subsidiary to the Legislative Building had the same controlled cornice line and height. The Legislative Building's roof profile moved slightly above them and toward the central dome, reinforcing the building's dominance. Ground lines, terraces, stairs, and ramps were similarly manipulated to indicate their supporting roles.

The handling of the dome and its relationship to the balance of the scheme called for some deftness. This was the essence of the design problem: to create a domed legislative building in harmony with the other campus structures and yet sufficiently scaled to be the central presence of the group as a whole. This problem was to return later and require a major adjustment in the plan.

Accepted designs, group plan and Temple of Justice elevations, Wilder and White, architects

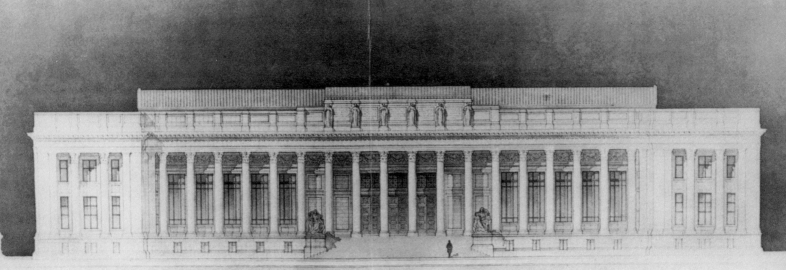

The Wilder and White dome in their drawings for the competition is only dimly seen, but its appearance suggests contemporary prototypes, especially Cass Gilbert's Minnesota State Capitol (1896), Joseph Huston's Pennsylvania State Capitol (1902), and Tracy and Swartwout's Missouri State Capitol (1913) (see page 96). All four owed more than a little to Michelangelo's St. Peter's. But unlike their Roman prototype, these domes rose freestanding above the building mass without the subsidiary domed tourelles of St. Peter's. Since at this stage of the competition no further indication was required of the contestants, there is no other evidence of what the partners had in mind for their Legislative Building.

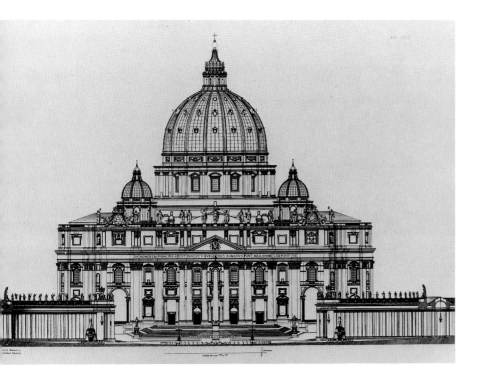

St. Peter's Basilica, Rome

Their Temple of Justice drawings, required by the competition program to be more detailed and at larger scale, are easier to examine. Matching the longitudinal dimensions of the Legislative Building, toward which its main entrance faced in the group plan, the Temple of Justice was shown as a long rectangular building with shallow extended wings at either end. Its proportions were horizontal, with an almost uninterrupted skyline and subdued ornamentation that would dampen any competition with the authority of the Legislative Building. The only challenges to this restraint were the use of the Corinthian order along the full length of both the north and south elevations and some sculptural emphasis at the main entrance. The interior plan mirrored the exterior symmetry with almost total balance of spaces on either side of the transverse axis.

Second Prize design, Howells and Stokes, architects

It is interesting to compare the Wilder and White entry with that of Howells and Stokes of New York, the winners of the second prize. The latter's vocabulary is much richer, heavier—and more costly. The principal departure from the Wilder and White scheme was the location of the Temple of Justice, placed south of the Legislative Building instead of north. This had the advantage of emphasizing the Legislative Building as the major building on the axial approach from the north. But it would have withdrawn almost half of the site's buildable area from use, creating a rather tight grouping of buildings on the southern portion of the site and requiring more state land acquisition in an already developed residential area for the location of the Governor's Mansion, while leaving portions of the existing site to the north dramatically open but extravagantly empty.

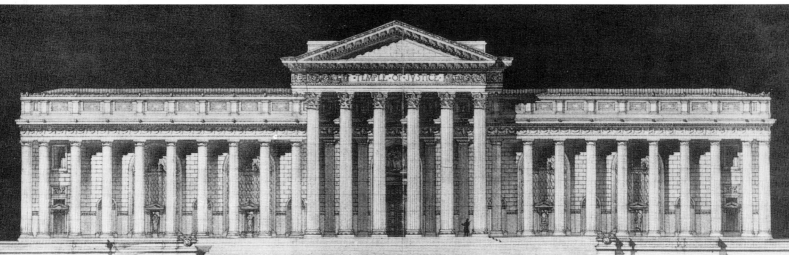

A similar extravagance is evident in the architectural handling. The overall impression is one of might: massive forms, heavy lights and shadows, the rich play of details, and a powerful porticoed entrance to the Legislative Building superimposed by a great square base with supporting tourelles and a rather horizontal dome that spectacularly dominates the group. It is a dome similar to Wilder and White's but much more squat in proportions. There is an undeniable power in this proposal, but somehow it seems overblown and out of scale with the ambitions and circumstances of the state. Perhaps the jury thought so, too.

In sum, Wilder and White had developed a scheme that suggested an incremental and orderly plan of development, worked well as ensemble in the architectural language of its day, and reflected a realistic appraisal of the promising but conservative economic goals of the clients.

One can still appreciate why the jury and commissioners would be attracted to this entry and give it their unanimous approval. Yet, though accepting the jury's choice, one cannot avoid wondering about its flaws. First, there are the difficult topographic realities of the site. Loftily located to maximum visual advantage above Puget Sound and the city with an uninterrupted axial orientation due north, nevertheless its bluffs made access from that direction both complex and enormously expensive.

Second Prize design, Howells and Stokes, architects

It was the competition program, however, which raised the issue, not the architects. The program states: "An axis developed through the center of the building north and south shall be the main or principal axis in the grouping plan." Further on it adds that the "Capitol Building faces the north," and "It is presumed that the main approaches to the Capitol Building and groups will be from the north and east," finally observing that "The best view is looking due north from the center of the proposed Capitol Building, which gives on Puget Sound."[2] The reality of the matter, though, is that any functional "main entrance" from the north would be likely to fail. Not only was the topography forbidding and soil conditions unstable but the area was occupied by one of Olympia's railroad stations and its yards; all these factors were calculated to complicate any effort to create an access to the campus by stairs and roadways.

Nevertheless, all the contestants of whom we have any record made gestures toward accommodating the commissioners' wishes for a north axial arrangement, doing so with various combinations of plazas, terraces, stairs, and ramps. With a single exception they offered variations of buildings grouped in U-shaped configurations whose arms opened without interruption to the northward vista. It was Wilder and White who chose to block that vista by their location of the Temple of Justice across its axis. We know, however, that even after the award had been made there were questions remaining in the minds of the commissioners and others about this aspect of the program which they had imposed on the competition. The State Archives has a typewritten "Report of Group Plan" addressed to the commission, dated August 29, 1911, and signed by Wilder and White, in answer to a query from the commission as to the architects' attitudes toward this requirement, now that the award was in hand and they could presumably respond more openly.

Wilder, who was in Olympia to accept the award, remained supportive of an approach from the north. His rationale, however, was more subjective than objective, the designer rather than the functionalist at work. The alternative had been suggested that the primary access to the campus might be westward from Main Street (now Capitol Way). In the architects' report, Wilder labeled this a route of only "accidental importance . . . starting nowhere and ending indefinitely." The route would be only two blocks long, and its prolongation east of Main Street "would have no reasonable justification." He further noted that to face the group plan east would be to "turn its back upon one of the most beautiful sections of the city"—West Olympia, across Budd Inlet from the site.

Even more unfortunate, continued Wilder, would be the dissociation of the site from its water views, which would be entirely cut off. Finally, he felt city growth should be encouraged westward rather than south or east; to focus the site plan in those latter directions would simply encourage the least promising areas for Olympia's future development.

Instead, concluded Wilder, the city should move toward providing

a fine boulevard . . . connecting the three distinctive ridges contained in the city limits, and giving access to the coast towns. On the axis of the capitol a fine approach from this boulevard to the foot of the steps would be made with a carriage approach on either side, and a boulevard to Tumwater along the water's edge there connecting with the proposed Pacific Highway. . . . A tide lock at the Boulevard [to the west] would form a lake* and the whole effect would be visible from most parts of the city as well as from the sound.

*A lake was developed in this way, but not until the early 1950s.

His boulevard would also "facilitate the natural travel through the city and direct it past the most beautiful portions," bypassing the city's south end while providing the fullest opportunity for visually exploiting the Capitol's site.

Most of Olympia's subsequent history and urban growth were to prove him mistaken. In spite of the scorn in which he held Main Street and the south end, it was on that route and in this section that the city growth and its better addresses predominated, at least until the advent of suburbanization after the Second World War, when development became multidirectional. The northern approach boulevard was thwarted by more dispassionate heads and the formidability of the site; even as a concept it would eventually disappear, thereby preserving for all time a group plan oriented north but approached from the east, a dichotomy never to be resolved, either then or in subsequent efforts by others.

The commissioners also had second thoughts about the advisability of retaining the Flagg foundations, and here Wilder was more circumspect. For the time being he simply observed in this same report to the commission that letting "the final result be marred by parsimony at this time would be most unfortunate. A proper answer. . . can only be made after a detail[ed] study."

Accepting, then, Wilder's enthusiasm for a northern orientation for the group plan, further questions remain: Why, unlike other contestants, did Wilder and White choose to confuse the Legislative Building's access to that northern vista with the transverse alignment of the Temple of Justice? And why do so when at the same time the axis to the south was being architecturally framed—but into an area which Wilder himself claimed had no distinctive visual amenities and which was composed of substantial privately owned residences? Why were the relationships of the accessory buildings of the group not reversed, closing the south axis with the Temple of Justice and dramatizing the axis to the north by framing its uninterrupted thrust with the pair of angled buildings? Were the partners questioned on this decision? Was it discussed by the jury or with the commissioners? The official records provide no enlightenment. However, information recently discovered in the Library of Congress Manuscript Division (discussed in Chapter 4) suggests that these questions had indeed been forced upon the commissioners' and architects' attention—but from a once-removed source.

But in 1911 the emphasis was on technicalities and timing. Although there were calls for further thought to protect site-planning principles and to prevent what they considered a violation of visual rules, the momentum of events swept them aside. The consequences can be seen in Olympia today.

It is a pity that White's letter to Miss Fitz Randolph, announcing the firm's triumph, has not survived. We know from those letters that do that he continued working on other projects in the office* while Wilder was in Olympia accepting the award and answering the questions of the State Capitol Commission. And so began what was to be an eighteen-year contractual association between Wilder and White and the State of Washington.

*White was busy finishing up presentations for the Plainfield Library competition, which the firm won a few weeks after their Olympia triumph.

IV. The Interim Years: 1911–1920

The competition for the Washington State Capitol may have been settled in 1911, but it was another eleven years before the Legislative Building, the centerpiece of the Wilder and White group plan, began to rise. The interim years saw successive restudies (especially of the dome and its role in the group plan), a critical period that brought the state to the brink of the plan's abandonment, and initial construction of peripheral buildings.

When the state announced the results of the competition on August 3, 1911, the commission also wired Olmsted Brothers of Brookline, Massachusetts—then the foremost landscape firm in the country—inquiring as to whether they could "prepare plans for Capitol Building grounds." No newcomers to the Pacific Northwest, the firm had been employed in Seattle since 1903 on major projects: the Seattle Park Plan, a plan for the University of Washington campus, the plan for the 1909 Alaska-Yukon-Pacific Exposition (whose framework still dominates the university's campus), plans for Woodland Park and Volunteer Park, and a generous scattering of other public and private work. Just after the commission's formation, there had been a recommendation* that the firm be employed as landscape consultants, and by invitation of Governor Hay the senior partner, John C. Olmsted, had made a preliminary visit to the Olympia site on April 13, 1911. Thus, when in August the Olmsteds were formally invited to become the commission's consultants, they quickly accepted. Thereafter, J. F. Dawson, an associate member of Olmsted Brothers, met with the commission in Olympia. On December 5, Dawson reported to his firm that at the meeting no mention was made of the Wilder and White group plan, and that the commission's top priority was "just the location of the temple of Justice so the architects could proceed with the plan and locate it properly." It is clear that the Olmsteds expected to play a central role in the development of the final design for the site, since there was still considerable flexibility.

There followed some weeks of restudy, resulting in their alternative proposal, dated January 18, 1912. The location of the Legislative Building on the Flagg foundations remained, now with an axial avenue stretching from the building's north facade (in a direct diagonal six blocks northeasterly to connect with the downtown business district at Main Street) and an existing park block facing the old Capitol Building. A subsidiary approach was added from Main Street due west to a monumental plaza before the south front of the Legislative Building. Opposite the latter, closing the plaza to the south, was a relocated Temple of Justice. Olmsted letters, to the commission and to Wilder and White, explained these plans at various stages of their development. But despite the apparent persuasiveness of their rationale for these revisions (especially with regard to the location for the Temple of Justice), the brothers failed to move either the commission or the architects, and the issue soon led to their dismissal.

With hindsight, it is possible to explain this deadlock. At the time of Wilder's visit to Olympia to meet with the commission and see the site, he was asked that final drawings for the group plan be prepared and submitted to the commission in six months, so that the location of the Temple of Justice could be settled and work proceed on this first building of the new group. Wilder was also asked to suggest possible revisions for the group plan as a whole, addressing questions raised concerning site orientation.

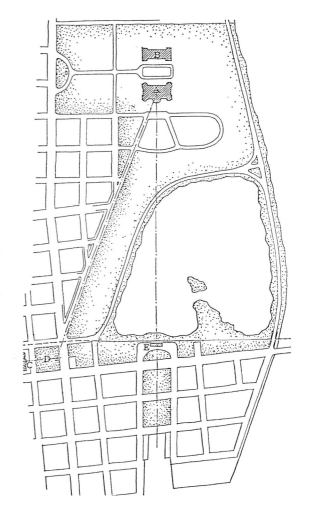

Olmsted Brothers site plan, 1912
A Legislative Building
B Temple of Justice
C Old capitol building
D City park
E Railroad station

Through the efforts of Charles W. Saunders, a Seattle architect. Saunders's letters of March 31, 1911, to John C. Olmsted implies that he took this initiative at Olmsted's request (Olmsted Brothers papers).

Until recently, little evidence has been available to clarify what the tone and content of those reconsiderations might have been. The commission minutes did not record them, and Wilder and White's end of the dialogue was lost along with their files on the Olympia work. However, new research among the Olmsted Brothers papers substantially clarifies what the commission and Wilder and White had in mind in their approach to the group plan.

When the announcement of the award of prizes for the 1911 competition was made, there had been the additional note that the Olmsteds were being hired in an advisory role to the commission. John C. Olmsted from the first had been troubled by what he saw. His detailed notes of his April visit, along with letters and telegrams both sent and received, shed light not only on his own concerns, but also on the rationale of the commission and the architects for what in due course was decided for the site. Out of Olmsted's efforts through the rest of 1911 came a plan which he sent to the commission, correcting what he saw as the major weaknesses of the Wilder and White plan. In his letter of transmittal, dated January 18, 1912, he expained that

> We are sending you under separate cover by mail prints of our alternative plans for the improvement of the Capitol grounds, based on the assumption that the Temple of Justice will be located south of the Capitol. . . . we request that your Commission give earnest and full consideration to the fundamental question whether it is advisable to hide or "blanket" the future Capitol building in various views from the City by locating the Temple of Justice north of the Capitol. We believe it would be a great mistake to do so. . . . It will inevitably produce the impression in the minds of most observers that the Temple of Justice is the important monumental building and that the Capitol is merely an incidental building or side show. . . .
>
> We desire to call particular attention to our suggestion that a diagonal avenue be laid out extending from the west part of the public square between Main Street and the temporary Capitol building to the front of the new Capitol building, centering on the dome. We believe such an avenue would be of immense value, not only for the desirable esthetic effect of connectng the Capitol directly with the business and park center of the City, hotels, railroad station, etc., but also as an obvious and sensible direct approach to the Capitol. Such an avenue will, of course, take more or less private property, which will be expensive, but we believe it will be worth all it will cost.

Olmsted's belief was not shared by the commission, however, and although it had reopened the matter, it was not willing to reconsider the location of the Temple of Justice.

A letter from the commission to Olmsted, dated January 21, 1912, reveals not only a number of factors which served as the basis for its decisions, but also the biases behind the group plan award to Wilder and White: the commission was still committed to the reuse of the Flagg foundations. The space between those foundations and the site's southern boundary line was thought insufficient to permit a generous plaza and site for the second most important building in the group plan, the Temple of Justice, without crowding the adjoining private properties. Furthermore, the commission did not have the legal authority (nor did it wish to go to the legislature to get it) for further land acquisition in that area, which was already under private development.

But one suspects that, in addition, the commissioners and their chosen architects were set on the original award-winning group plan. Having that already in hand, and being pressed for time to complete drawings and bidding and to begin construction of the Temple before appropriation authorizations ran out, the commission viewed the Olmsted initiative as disruptive and gratuitous. Thus, with some asperity, the commission concluded its response to the Olmsted firm by asking for a billing for its services and severing relations with it. So, for the time being, the case was rested, and on February 27, 1912, the commission, again by unanimous consent, approved a revised *Wilder and White* plan and adopted it as the "Group System of Buildings for the State."[1] This was not, however, to be the final version of the group plan or of the Legislative Building which was to dominate it; one sees the sequence in a publication record at four different stages in its evolution. The first-stage plan was the one presented at the time of the competition in 1911 and published in the September 13, 1911, issue of *The American Architect*. This was followed by the 1912 plan, described in an article written by the architects and published in *The American Architect* in 1915.[2] Next are drawings of 1920, when the partners began final studies for the Legislative Building but continued to adhere to the Flagg foundations. And finally, there is the series of construction drawings of the early 1920s on which Legislative Building construction was specifically based. By following the changes shown in these plans through those years, inferences can be made as to the evolutionary process leading to the building and group plan as they exist today.

The group plan for 1912 shows no significant departure from the plan of 1911. It reaffirmed the location of the Temple of Justice and the other buildings of the group and their relationship to the Flagg foundations, on which the Legislative Building was to rise. There were some alterations to the shoreline configuration to permit a more dramatic and extended approach to the site from the north, along a landscaped esplanade closed by a triumphal arch* centered in another roundpoint and leading to a double-ramped ascent to the terraces above. The monumental staircase of 1911 disappeared, the likely result of Wilder's having personally observed the severe topographic reality of the site. Also gone was the outdoor amphitheater, dropped from the program. Otherwise, the original group plan relationship of the seven buildings (including the Governor's Mansion) was retained.

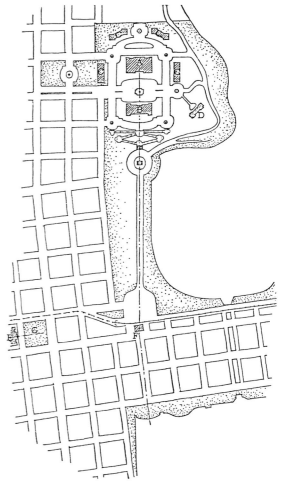

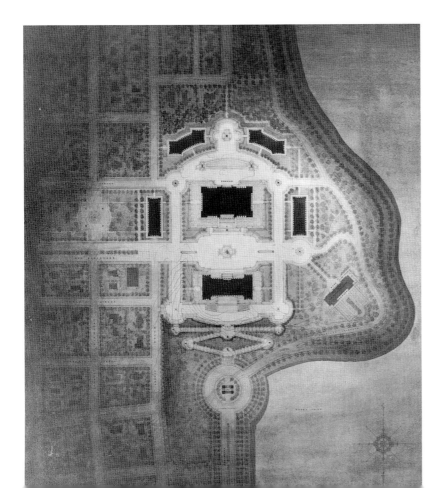

Revised Wilder and White site plan, 1912
A *Legislative Building*
B *Temple of Justice*
C *Administrative buildings*
D *Governor's Mansion*
E *Old capitol building*
F *Railroad station*
G *City park*

Howell and Stokes had included an arch in their competition drawings, in the same location.

The revised group plan, 1912

Important changes are to be found, however, in a revised elevation and especially in perspective studies that were the result of the six additional months given the architects for refinement of their competition presentation. The focus shows that the partners were preoccupied with a single element: the dome. This is reminiscent of Ware's evaluation of designs submitted for the 1893 competition, when he observed in his report to the commission that the domes were often the weakest element of the entries and a clue to the competence of their designers.

When Wilder and White came to work on their own dome, American architects had been developing a repertoire of experience in handling this supreme element in the architectural vocabulary considerably beyond the more tentative record of the 1890s. By the beginning of the First World War there had been completed some splendid precedents. Thus, the partners were able to draw from such well-publicized state capitol domes as those of Minnesota (Cass Gilbert), Rhode Island (McKim, Mead and White), Mississippi (Theodore C. Link), Kentucky (Frank Andrews), Pennsylvania (Joseph Huston), Wisconsin (George B. Post and Son), Utah (Richard Kletting), and Missouri (Tracy and Swartwout), as well as the San Francisco City Hall (Arthur Brown, Jr.). All were completed before the design for the Olympia dome was finally settled.

The partners' dome in their competition drawings had been conventionally handled, with clear visual ties to the domes of Minnesota and Pennsylvania. In the six-month restudy, however, Wilder and White must have felt some urge to give the dome increased dominance and more individualized design.

The 1912 revised group plan, elevation from north

Their 1912 drawings offer both. The dome's overall height was increased, leaving no question about where the design balance was to lie:

The 1912 revised group plan perspective

In its mass it is apparent the Group Plan responds primarily to the necessity of so arranging a collection of small units that they may combine to give the effect of a single structure when viewed from a distance and from all directions. Hence, the Legislative Building, slightly larger than the others and surmounted by a lofty dome, occupies the center of the group. The Temple of Justice is directly north across the Court of Honor and the four Commission Buildings are grouped on either side and to the south. The simple colonnaded treatment of these surrounding buildings will from a distance tend to make them appear as a single broad base to the central dome.[3]

More apparent, however, are the changes introduced in the design of the dome itself. The circular plan was discarded, replaced by a two-part scheme. The lower level was a modified and colonnaded octagon with greater width given to the cardinal elevations. This, in turn, was superimposed by the dome itself, an octagon whose transition at the drum was eased by large volutes at each corner. The design is not without precedent. Did White's love of Italy and his travel there remind him of Brunelleschi's octagonal dome in Florence? A similar idea had been proposed at one stage in the development of the New York Capitol in the 1870s, but there was no precedent in this country to encourage its use in Olympia. Second thoughts would come, but for now the architects were preoccupied with the design and construction of accessory buildings on the campus. Further study of the Legislative Building would have to wait.

At one point in the development of the Wilder and White plans for the capitol group history almost repeated itself—shades of Governor Rogers and the Flagg building at the turn of the century. A change of administration brought a new governor to the chair of the commission: Ernest Lister, who in 1913 succeeded Governor Hay. The only Democrat in an otherwise entirely Republican administration, Lister had been elected on a platform of economy and businesslike management for state affairs; his attention was soon drawn to the ambitious and conspicuous project of the state capitol.

Convinced of the extravagance of the 1912 group plan, he was particularly disturbed by its north-south orientation, preferring instead an approach from due east. For the rest of the decade—while planning and construction of the Temple of Justice proceeded—the commission, the legislature, the state's architects, and the press grappled off and on with the issue. The commission supported the governor's alternative plan; the legislature vacillated, at one time denying the commission the authority for such drastic rethinking but later granting it; and the architects, led by Charles Bebb, were united in their opposition to this abandonment of the "vision, ideals, and dignity" (Bebb's words) of the Wilder and White group plan. The architects were supported by both the *Seattle Post-Intelligencer* and the *Seattle Star.*

But before any construction obligated the commission to make a permanent commitment to the Lister plan, a shifting of priorities and rising costs due to the dislocation of World War I caused a postponement of building activity on the site. The end of the war, the death of Lister (in 1919), a new governor and chairman (Louis F. Hart, a Republican), and more rethinking of the issue by the commission finally resulted in a renewed commitment to the partners' group plan. Thus the question of the capitol's site plan disappeared from the commission's agendas.

In the meantime both the commission and the architects had been occupied with activity whose progress had not been interrupted by the background disturbances of the continuing group plan debate. The commission at its February 17, 1912, meeting had turned its attention to the matter of construction of the first unit of the plan, the Temple of Justice, whose design had also been awarded to Wilder and White. Until 1925, when the legislature

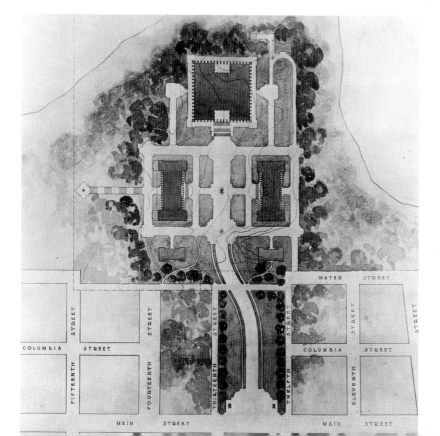

The Lister group plan, 1915

made certain changes in the administration of capitol construction funding, special direct tax levies were required as loans to the capitol building fund. In a singularly ungenerous gesture toward the project's beginning stages, the legislature authorized work on the Temple of Justice but with funding that was far short of what was necessary. The commission therefore authorized the architects to prepare the building for occupancy by the state supreme court, the Law Library, and the offices of the attorney general, with partial completion of the interior but leaving the exterior for later appropriations. Construction was done on this basis. Both the 1913 and 1915 legislative sessions included money issues for the additional funding, but in each case the authorizing language was declared by the state supreme court to be unconstitutional. It was not until 1917 that the legislature solved the constitutional questions, releasing $350,000 to give the raw brick exterior walls and stripped interior spaces of the Temple of Justice their present appearance.

The architects were now confronted with two important policy issues related both to the Temple of Justice and to future units of the group. The first had to do with finish materials. There were several sources of stone in the state in relatively easy access to Olympia. Chuckanut stone from Whatcom County quarries on northern Puget Sound had been used for the Thurston County Courthouse. It is robust and durable but rather forbidding in its gray tones, especially when washed by the Puget Sound rain, and was quite out of fashion in contemporary monumental construction, which favored more finish brilliance. Tenino stone from the southern part of Thurston County has much the same qualities as the Chuckanut stone. Wilkeson stone from quarries in neighboring Pierce County is quite different. A sandstone of durability similar to those of the other stones, its colors are in notable contrast to their sobriety: light, warm, off-white tones with shadings of pale cream and hints of pink. On sunny days it is light but not harsh, nor does it turn gloomy on gray days or in the rain. Finally, it was available in quantities sufficient to supply the entire group through the years of construction. Wilkeson stone was therefore the choice of the architects and the commissioners.

Temple of Justice before installation of stone facing, ca. 1919

A design question also remained to be solved. The budget was insufficient to complete the Temple of Justice as originally designed, and the architects were asked to make adjustments. They recommended replacing the ornate (and expensive) Corinthian order on the exterior colonnades and pilasters with the simpler Roman Doric order. The commission agreed to the alternative in July 1917, not only for the first unit of the group plan but— by implication, for purposes of unity—for the future peripheral buildings of the group as well. But by the end of the year the nation was at war. It was therefore decided to confine work to the most essential: the stone facing of the exterior walls. Interior finishing awaited the end of the war. The Temple of Justice was finally accepted by the state in August 1920 at a total cost of $942,230.

Construction in the early 1920s prior to turning to the Legislative Building included two additional buildings. Drawing from a $2,500,000 construction fund established by the 1919 legislature, the commission authorized Wilder and White to prepare plans for a general office building to the east of the Legislative Building site. This was in response to the increasing space needs of state government and the pressures they exerted on the inadequate downtown capitol. The Insurance Building, as it was to be named, was less monumental than the Temple of Justice though it resembled the earlier building in key features (Wilkeson stone and Roman Doric order). Begun early in 1920 and costing $1,032,000, it was occupied in 1921 by miscellaneous state offices including that of the governor.

For a site below the west bluffs and out of sight on the tidelands, Wilder and White also designed a central powerhouse and heating plant for the campus, completed in 1920. Utilities are distributed to the various units by a large distribution tunnel system.[4]

*Walter R. Wilder, architect
(work on Temple of Justice in progress)*

Temple of Justice and Insurance Building, ca. 1921

The Capitol campus power and heating plant, ca. 1920

The Legislative Building thus still lay ahead, and in a final act to clarify the administrative means for progressing toward its construction, the governor included the commission in his proposals for reform of the state's Civil and Administrative Code. In 1921, the State Capitol Commission of seven members was replaced by a new and leaner State Capitol Committee of only three members: the governor, the state auditor, and the state land commissioner.[5] This was the committee that would be responsible for seeing the centerpiece of the state's capitol group completed. Now began the work that would continue throughout the 1920s.

The State Capitol Commission and others, August 11, 1920. Left to right: Charles H. Bebb, architect; Fred G. Cook, assistant secretary, State Capitol Commission; C. W. Clausen, state auditor; Clark V. Savidge, state land commissioner; Governor Louis F. Hart; Harry Whitney Treat; Henry McCleary; A. H. Chambers.

The Capitol Committee and others, probably at the Legislative Building topping-out ceremonies, October 13, 1926. Left to right: unknown; P. H. Carlyon, Thurston County state senator; Clark V. Savidge, state land commissioner; Walter R. Wilder, architect; C. W. Clausen, state auditor; Governor Roland H. Hartley.

V. The Construction Years

The design and construction decade of the 1920s centered on the Legislative Building and featured a cast of participants that remained almost unchanged to the building's completion. Representing the state was the State Capitol Committee. This new three-man body was granted a remarkable degree of autonomy in its management of the Capitol lands and the income derived from their timbers. Once funding arrangements were authorized, the legislature and, indeed, the people of the state were hardly more than interested observers of the committee's actions in matters that ranged from questions of building placement to selection of rugs and furniture.

The committee's members were, however, elected officials whose primary duties lay elsewhere. The chairman was Governor Hart, later to be replaced by Governor Hartley. The secretary was Clark V. Savidge, the state land commissioner, and the third member was C. W. Clausen, the state auditor. Indirect participants in the concerns of the committee were J. Grant Hinkle, the secretary of state, and John H. Dunbar, the attorney general. Neither had an officially designated role in committee affairs but both were often drawn into its discussions—and later, its squabbles.

The architects, of course, were Wilder and White. Wilder was almost always the partner representing the firm in Olympia, making frequent and extended visits during the building's construction. He also established some personal associations with Olympia people unconnected with the work and enjoyed social functions, legislative balls, golfing, and recreational visits in the region. He is remembered by one Olympian as a not particularly talkative man, perhaps somewhat lonely, but competent and thorough.[1] By contrast, White visited no more than one or two times while work was in progress, though in later years he made a number of sentimental visits to the finished building.

More on-site architectural presence was established by the partners in two ways. The commission had authorized them to form an association with the Seattle architectural office of Bebb and Gould. Charles H. Bebb, the former commission expert, was its principal representative. His role was administrative and advisory at those times when Wilder was not in Olympia. In addition, Jay Johnston was the permanent representative of the architects on the job and responsible for its field progress. Although referred to by a number of titles including "superintending architect," his background and experience were as a building and construction supervisor. His business card identified him as the "representative" of the architects and associate architects. A native of Wisconsin, he had been living in Seattle but came to Olympia perhaps as early as 1919 in connection with the finishing work on the Temple of Justice. By 1921 he was working out of the architects' field office, which had been assigned them in a corner of the Temple's ground floor. Olympia became his permanent home.

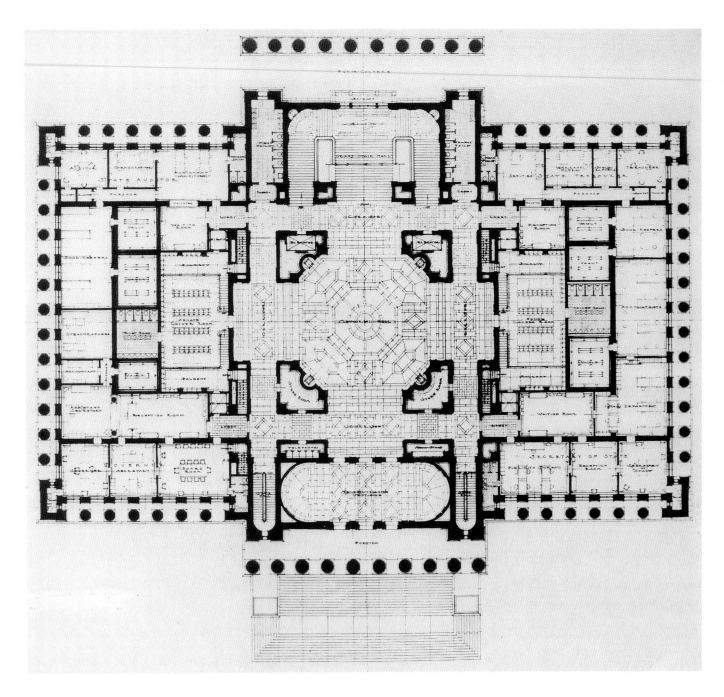

The contracts for construction of the Legislative Building were held by two firms at separate times. Largely for financial and legislative management reasons, construction was in three phases: the foundations and first floor, continuation of the building to the base of the dome, and the dome itself. Pratt and Watson of Tacoma was the general contractor for the first phase; the same firm had also built the Insurance Building. Sound Construction and Engineering Company of Seattle won the general contracts for the final two phases. There were often three hundred or more men working at the time of heaviest activity during the five or so years of construction.

First floor plan of the 1920 preliminary drawings for the Legislative Building based on the Flagg foundations

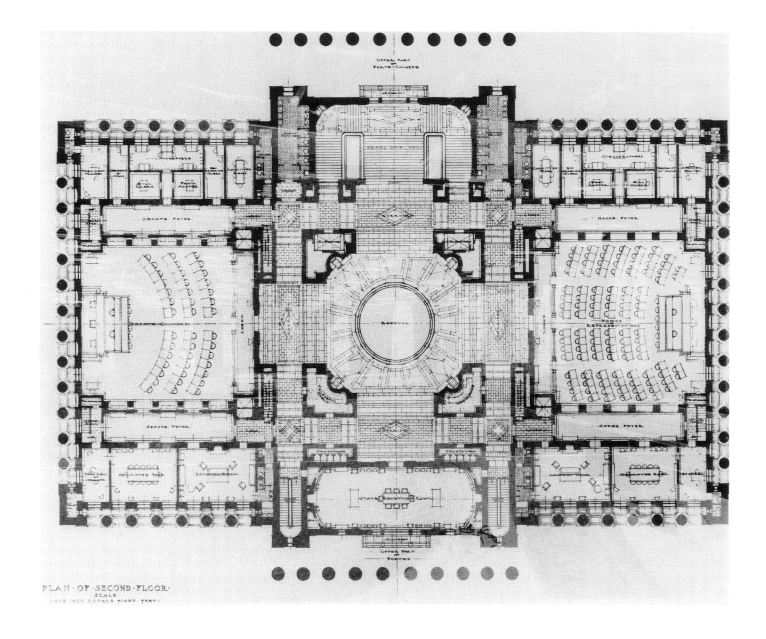

PLAN·OF·SECOND·FLOOR·
·SCALE·
·ONE INCH EQUALS EIGHT FEET·

Although the actual breaking of ground for the Legislative Building did not take place until 1922, the architects had begun their work in preparation for that event in 1920. After Governor Hart took office but while the seven-member commission was still the responsible agency, Wilder and White had written the commission at its request on September 21, 1920, explaining the results of their further study of the building with an accompanying set of drawings. So far as can be told from existing records, this was the first time that the architects had been required to elaborate the building's interior plans and to interpret in explicit terms what heretofore had been either distant profile views of the dome or generalized exterior perspectives.

Second floor plan of the 1920 preliminary drawings for the Legislative Building based on the Flagg foundations

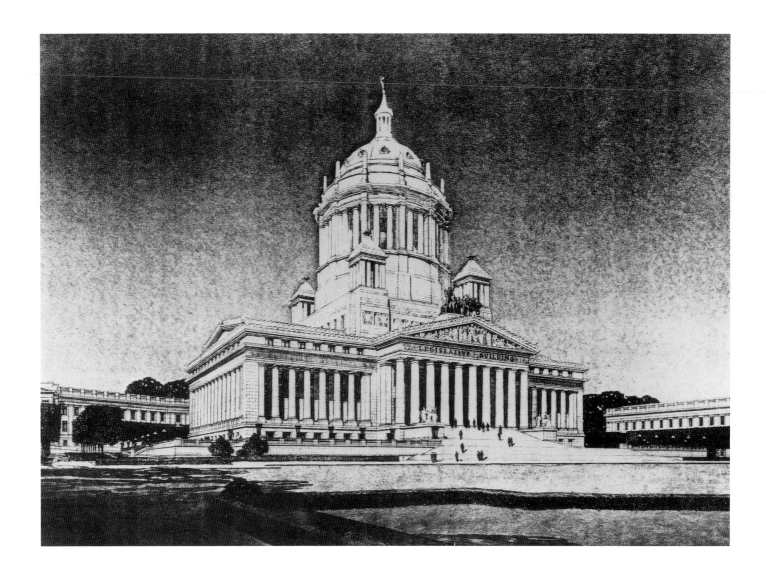

The partners' letter notes that the building would be "resting on the existing Flagg foundations" and describes internal arrangements which, other than the enforced compactness to fit within the foundations' dimensions and the handling of vertical circulation, are not unlike what one finds there today. The first floor with its centrally located Memorial Hall (approached on the north by monumental exterior stairs and from the south by interior stairs) contained offices for the governor, the secretary of state, the state treasurer, and the state auditor, and locker rooms for members of the Senate and House. The south stairs continued up from this level to the second floor and to a rotunda beneath the dome, with the Senate Chamber to the east and the House Chamber to the west, each with its own supporting offices and conference rooms. To the north of the rotunda was the State Reception Room.

Externally, the body of the building had much of the same spirit established in the 1912 revisions: a rectangular block, with colonnaded wings to the north and south and central colonnaded and pedimented entrance porticoes between. The order chosen for the columns was a simplified Roman Doric (no fluting). Their austerity was to be relieved by rich sculpture in the pediments and the cheneaux that decorated the building's cornice lines. An added fourth floor was managed by superimposing an attic story above the entablature of the colonnaded wings.

Perspective of the Legislative Building based on the Flagg foundations, 1920

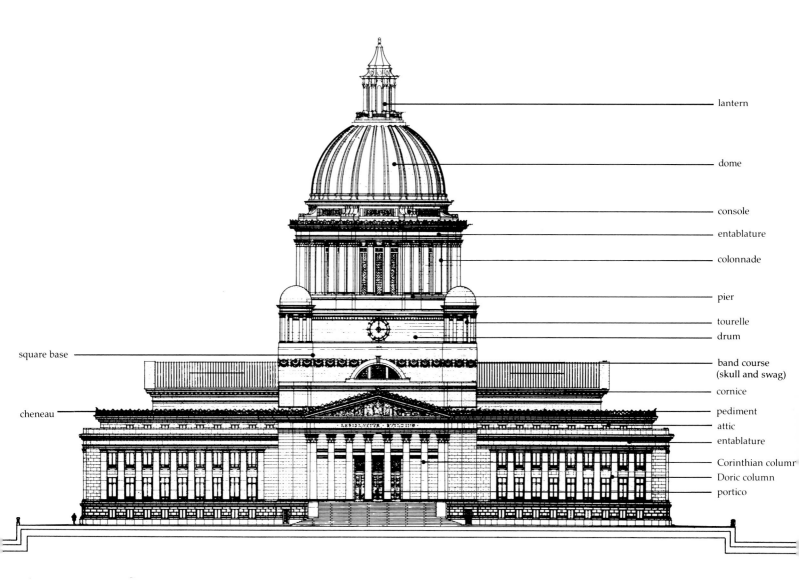

lantern

dome

console

entablature

colonnade

pier

tourelle

drum

square base

band course
(skull and swag)

cornice

cheneau

pediment

attic

entablature

Corinthian column

Doric column

portico

The dome, however, was subjected to a third set of revisions, this time benefiting from much more detailed examination given to the whole building. A series of study models had convinced the architects that the design called for a dome of not more but less height than that proposed in 1912. Twenty feet were eliminated. The architects also returned to a more conventional circular dome which rose from a central square base and a tall drum to provide the necessary height to dominate the group plan. It was a ribbed dome with a single line of lunettes. These and the obelisks that accented the dome's springline gave the ensemble a somewhat florid appearance. The partners rejected their earlier freestanding domes and adopted supporting tourelles at the four corners of the base, square in plan and topped by pyramids.

Though there would be further changes, notably in the treatment of the tourelles, the preliminary drawings of 1920 clearly set the tone for the final design.

Glossary of architectural terms

But the further the partners advanced into the Legislative Building's planning, the more troublesome became its inheritance of the Flagg foundations. Partly, it was their impact on the space assignments in the new building which were now seen as unsuitably cramped; "a considerable loss of dignity would result" from the unspacious dimensions of the executive offices. It was also a question of the composition of the group as a design entity; the foundations limited the building to a size which, as support for its dome, was visually inadequate to the task. Flagg's dome was only 150 feet high; the partners' was nearly twice that. Its proportional relationship to the group was thus ensured, but its mass would overwhelm the imposed modest scale of the structure immediately beneath it.

The only way to gain more space and reestablish balance between building and dome was to abandon the existing foundations, and at last this was agreed to by the new committee. Thus the building was allowed to adjust to its own conditions rather than those set for it in 1893; almost eighty feet of length and twenty feet of width were added to its plan.[2]

In 1921, discovering that there were still unspent funds that had been authorized for construction of the Insurance Building, the legislature approved their reassignment for first phase construction on the Legislative Building's foundations and first floor. In August, Wilder presented the committee with the partners' revised preliminary plans for the foundations, terraces, and walls of the first floor of the building. The committee approved the plans and instructed the architects "to proceed at once with the working drawings, to the intent and purposes that the State Capitol Committee may be able to advertise for bids for a portion of the Legislative Building for which funds may be available, approximately $500,000."[3]

On February 2, 1922, Wilder was back with the requested drawings and they were approved by the committee. He was then asked to prepare advertisements for bids and the contract with Pratt and Watson was signed on March 23, 1922.

Work began immediately, though the weather was unseasonal. Johnston reported to the partners as late as May 8 that the excavation work had to be stopped due to rain and snow. This also caused trouble for the pouring of the concrete footings, but by the end of the month he was reporting good progress both in the work in general and with the concrete pours.

Foundation wall granite from Index, Washington, and the structural and reinforcing steel were also arriving. The architects became rather apprehensive about the pace of some of the work. They wrote to Johnston on June 2 complaining that the stone suppliers

have gone ahead and gotten out practically all of the stone without waiting for any approval. Were they behind, this might have more justification, but to have all of the stone on the site so long before it will be required would seem to be only for the purpose of enabling Walker [of Walker Cut Stone Company, the Tacoma supplier of the Wilkeson stone] to get his payments early. We have no objection to this but we do not like to see it done at the expense of the building as is the present case.

John "Mack" MacIver, a Scotsman with an appropriate accent, was the chief stonemason on the job.

Earlier in the same letter they noted they had been placed in the position of approving work "which is not right and rely on its not being noticeable, not a proper attitude on work of this character." The partners consistently demanded the highest level of performance from those associated with them on the project. Johnston was satisfied that both the granite and the Wilkeson stone being trucked in from the quarries were "of very fine quality," but he warned Walker to continue to be careful in selection, "as he had told Mr. Wilder he would be." On July 26 he could report that

The work on the building is progressing very nicely and tomorrow will likely finish concrete for the main walls. Stone is practically all set on the south main wall of the building with a considerable amount of reserve for setting on east and west walls. Mack will start setting on these walls sometime this week.

In August the committee prepared for the official laying of the cornerstone in the northeast corner of the building, determining whom to invite and purchasing a suitable trowel. The ceremony took place on Saturday, September 1, and was conducted by the Grand Lodge of Masons of Washington under Grand Master James M. McCormack of Tacoma. The cornerstone had been designed to receive a copper box containing, among other things, the signatures of the Capitol Committee, the architects, and the contractors; various lodge membership listings; copies of the Olympia newspaper; names of invited civic and legislative leaders, and a copy of a Masonic address on the "Life of George Washington."[4]

Laying of the Legislative Building cornerstone, September 1, 1922. The text of the cornerstone reads:

Laid by the M W Grand Lodge of F and AM of Washington September 9 1922 A L 5922 / James McCormack Grand Master / State Capitol Committee Louis F Hart Governor / Clark V Savidge Commissioner of Public Lands / C W Clausen State Auditor Architects Wilder and White / Contractors Pratt and Watson

The winter of 1922–23 was unusually severe, with first rain and later snow and ice delaying construction. The general contractor and the stone suppliers in the quarries were at a standstill. Johnston wrote to Wilder and White on December 20, 1922:

I was in Tacoma yesterday to take up with Walker the question of December deliveries and also went to the quarry to see what the conditions were there. They started a few cutters yesterday on the stone for his contract. . . . They are still snowed under at the quarry and it will be several days before they are able to ship any stone. Even though the cold spell broke here on December 19th the water pipes were still frozen at the quarry and they were working a few men to get the water pipes thawed out in order to get the gang saws started today.

On January 13 he wrote to the partners again on the same subject:

We are having the most severe rains here that have been experienced in years with flooded areas in several parts of the state, but so far nothing of any consequence here except more delay of the present work which the Governor does not seem to be alarmed about in any way.

Nor was there any letup by mid-February:

You have no doubt seen by the papers that we are having very severe winter weather for this section of the country. The first part of the month we had freezing weather so that we could expect no stone and then our present snow storm came along and paralyzed everything so that to date we have only received two loads of stone this month, and the prospects are not very promising, for according to the weather reports, we may get more snow.

Nevertheless, Pratt and Watson managed somehow to maintain a work schedule with only limited delays, and at its February 9 meeting the committee formally accepted the firm's completed work. The stone company's handling of work and materials, however, was much more jeopardized by the severity of the weather. Johnston wrote to the architects on March 23 that "Mr. Walker has had a nervous breakdown and has been to California for a month, getting back a couple of days ago." On March 3 the thermometer had read "20 degrees above zero at 8 o'clock this morning, which is very cold for this time of year."

In the meantime, Wilder and White were proceeding with the construction drawings for the entire building, carrying them forward as far as possible in anticipation of the 1923 session of the legislature. They had been urged to do so by the committee to win the legislature's authorization of the next phase of construction. Full sets of these drawings began to appear in the records by March 1923, with minor design changes in the later sets.

These drawings demonstrated the opportunities that had been opened to the architects by the abandonment of the Flagg foundations. There was, of course, more room on each floor for added offices; for example, the two legislative chambers could each have offices on three rather than only two sides. More significant, however, were changes in vertical circulation. Instead of the interior stairs south of the rotunda, as in the 1920 drawings, the rotunda itself served double duty. On the north-south axis, visitors would mount from the entrance floor to an intermediate ceremonial landing directly beneath the dome, where the state seal was imbedded in the marble floor. They would then turn either east or west for their ascent to the legislative floor—the Senate to the east, the House to the west.

The project thus moved into the 1923 legislative year, including the Capitol Bill for $2,000,000 of bond authorization, which passed both chambers without significant opposition. Wilder arrived in Olympia on April 1 to deliver the plans and specifications for Phase Two to the committee. Bidding did not proceed smoothly this time; all bids were rejected the first time around. But on August 1, 1923, contracts were signed with a new firm, the Sound Construction and Engineering Company of Seattle, for continuing the work. Colin Hastie, the company's vice-president, was in general charge of the job.

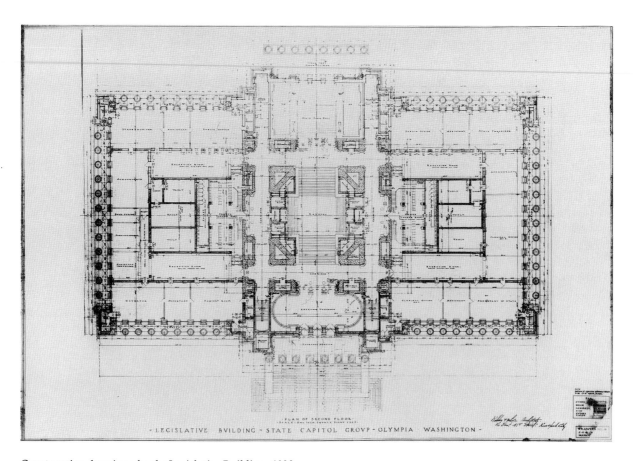

Second floor plan

Construction drawings for the Legislative Building, 1923

First floor plan

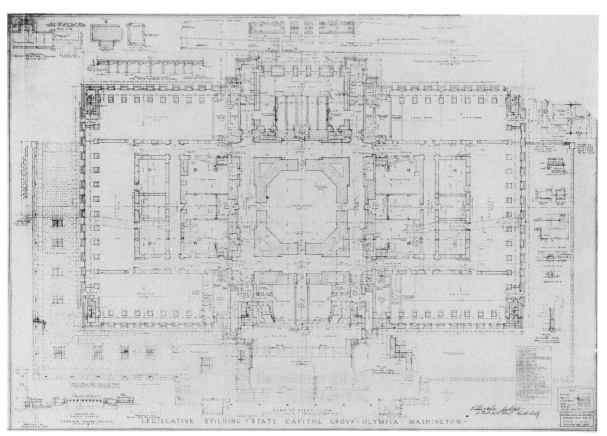

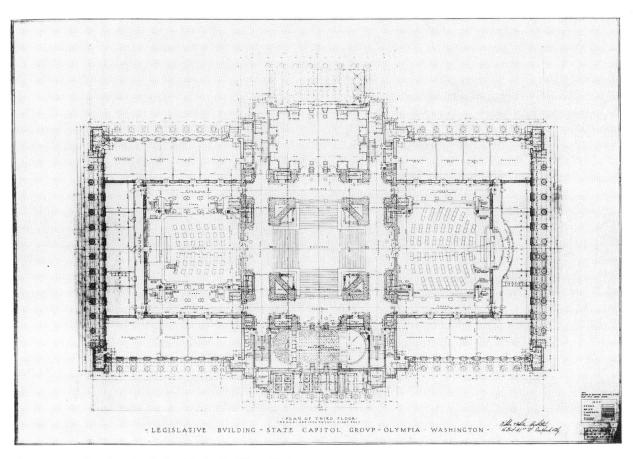

Third floor plan

Construction drawings for the Legislative Building, 1923

The state reception room

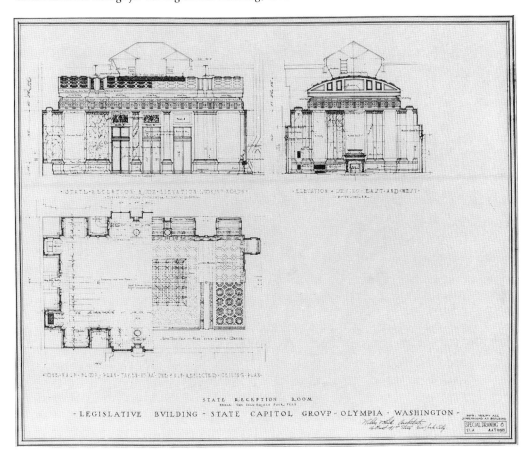

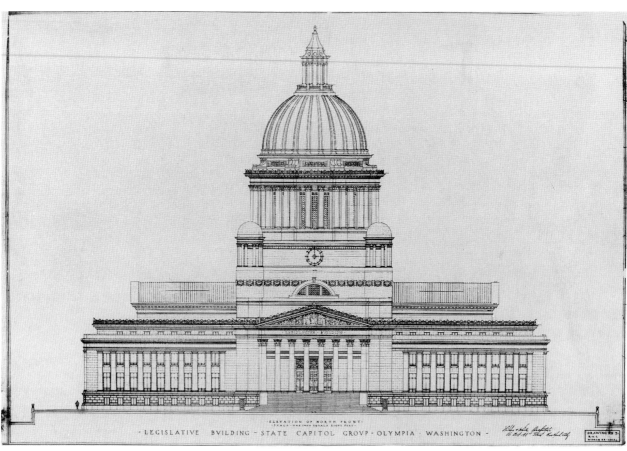

North elevation

Construction drawings for the Legislative Building, 1923

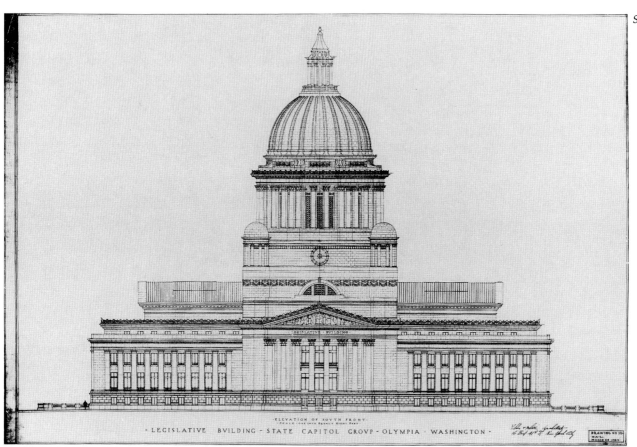

South elevation

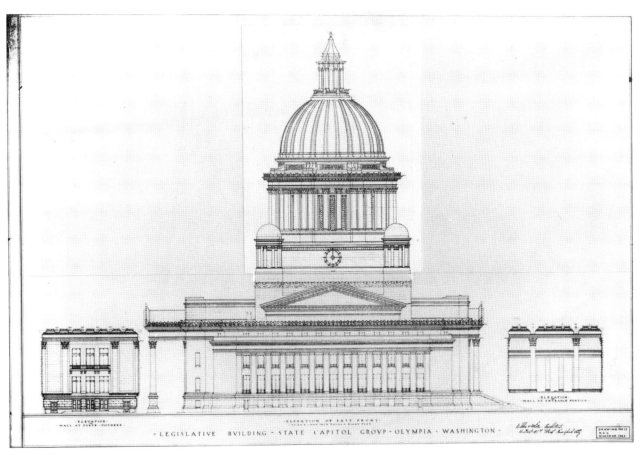

Construction drawings for the Legislative Building, 1923

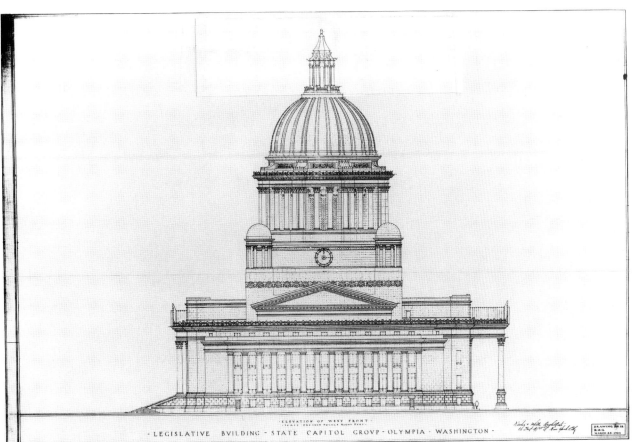

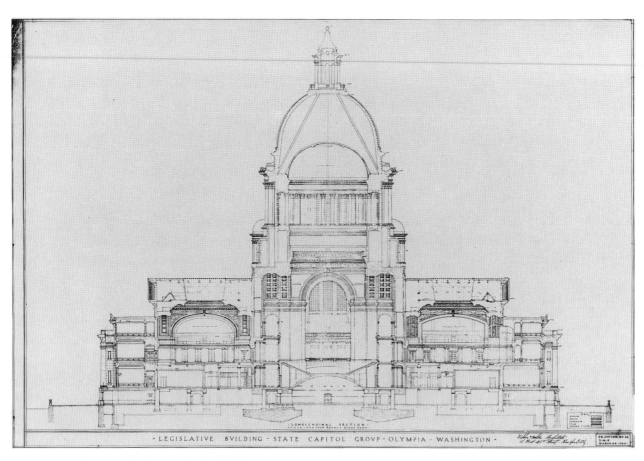

- LEGISLATIVE · BVILDING · STATE · CAPITOL · GROVP · OLYMPIA · WASHINGTON ·

Longitudinal section

Construction drawings for the Legislative Building, 1923

Transverse section

- LEGISLATIVE · BVILDING · STATE · CAPITOL · GROVP · OLYMPIA · WASHINGTON ·

58 *Washington's Audacious State Capitol*

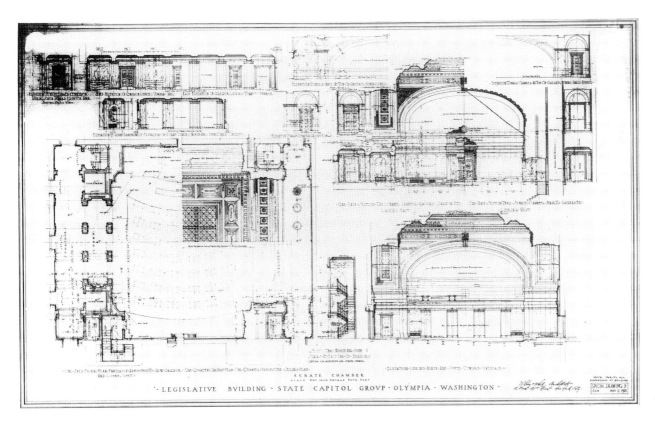

The Senate Chamber

Construction drawings for the Legislative Building, 1923

The House Chamber

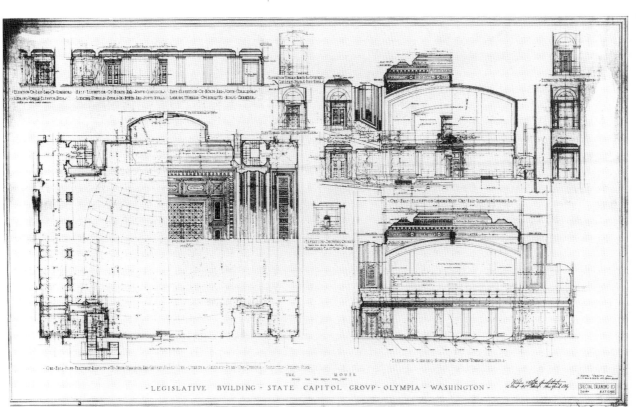

An undated letter from the partners to the new contractor, in Wilder's handwriting (perhaps this is a draft for later typing), illustrates the architects' attitude toward the project and their interest in drawing the contractor (whom they had not yet met) into similar commitments:

The committee is endeavoring to complete the building in the best possible manner at the lowest cost consistent therewith and your cooperation is essential to their success. We have sought the same end in our specifications but it is obvious that in work of this magnitude our lack of complete knowledge of local conditions opens the possibility for improvement and we shall be glad of suggestions from you at any time. Such suggestions will be given careful attention and will be appreciated even if our decision is against them.

Four [sic] considerations will govern as follows: First, better quality at the same cost; second, equal quality at less cost; third, expedition of the work without sacrifice of the quality. We should like the assurance that all of you will give careful consideration to any factor that may come up; will judge it on its merits in the light of your own experience; will forward to us any suggestions which in your judgment [are] valuable on any grounds mentioned; and above all allow the State the full saving in cost that may result. . . . In other words you will not be interfered with in the exercise of your personal judgment, unless special conditions arise.

We might add that this letter has been submitted to the Committee and expresses the views of the members.

As it developed, the association of the several parties involved proved to be an entirely satisfying one. Sound Construction was an excellent contractor; the work progressed smoothly and at a high standard of performance.

The first priority with the new work was to start clearing away those of the old foundations that were not being incorporated into the revised plans, and especially to prepare for the foundation work that would support the enormous piers and loads of the dome and its substructure. Autumn that year was more hospitable than winter had been, and this was especially important for keeping the subsoil of a large open pit dry for later concrete pouring. A mat of concrete, six inches deep and 130 feet square, was poured in mid-October to receive the dome foundation slab. This slab would be a monolith of concrete and reinforcing steel, 22'6" at its maximum depth, that was complex not only in design but also in the technology of its placement.* To ensure maximum cohesiveness, it had to be poured without interruption, a task that took four days and nights and was completed on November 2.

*Consulting engineers were the Gunvald Aus Company of New York City.

The sand and gravel came from Steilacoom. As the day approached for the pour, the contractors began shoving barges down the Sound, after the fashion of a commander putting an invading army ashore. Trucks labored up the streets, men fumed, perspired and swore. When the last form was in place and the service of supply began functioning in earnest, Hastie gave the word and the battle was on. It went for four days and nights. When the last bucket of material was dumped, Hastie slumped away to bed, unshaven and exhausted, but the base was one— Wilder and White, architects, had their solid piece of masonry.[5]

The rest of Phase Two was anticlimactic. Work proceeded smoothly through 1923 and 1924, with some snow at the turn of the year but nothing like the previous winter.

The stone rolled into the building in a never-ending procession. Stone cutters . . . carved and shaped it to fit into a dream which architects, working over drafting tables back in New York, had sketched on paper. They were fifteen months getting the stone in place.[6]

Progress photograph of construction, August 5, 1923. Note the remnants of brick wall from the old Flagg foundations.

Progress photograph of construction, October 16, 1923, showing steel work for the dome foundations

Progress photograph of construction, January 3, 1924. The framing at center is for a shallow vault over the cafeteria.

Progress photograph of construction, March 3, 1924

By the end of 1924 the exterior walls were essentially complete: twelve inches of stone facing together with brick or concrete backing for an overall thickness of 2′5″. All this finish stone had been precut with great accuracy at the plant in Tacoma before being trucked to Olympia. The detail drawings gave the specific dimensions for each piece, and each piece was coded as to location, a kind of enormous jigsaw puzzle. "[T]he smallest stone in the building could be lifted by a boy, and the largest stone weighs 18 tons. Between these two extremes are hundreds upon thousands of stones of varying weight and shape."[7] Late 1924 also saw the gables and roofs for the Senate and House chambers nearing completion, the square base for receiving the dome taking shape, and scaffolding being removed.

In October 1924 the architects were directed by the committee to proceed at once with plans and specifications for the completion of the Legislative Building. The 1925 legislative session authorized the Capitol Committee's $4,000,000 bond issue for construction of the dome and interior finishing of the building and thus the state was readied for this final effort.* The architectural drawings dated May 12, 1925, and pertaining specifically to the dome were back to the committee that month. In their transmittal letter of May 22 the partners noted: "The only changes have been in certain details of the dome after careful study of the plaster model, and these do not appreciably affect the cost."[8] On July 6 the contract was again awarded to Sound construction, in the amount of $3,167,060. It covered the construction of the dome, interior finishing, lighting and heating systems, elevators, and painting and wall hangings—in effect, it would put the building in complete readiness for furnishing and occupancy.[9]

It was also in January 1925 that Governor Hart was succeeded by Governor Roland H. Hartley, an executive change that would have important ramifications for the heretofore placid functioning of the committee.

All concerned could now turn their full attention to the capitol group's most complex structural element, the dome. In terms of both architectural history and the American art of building, domes occupy a special place in the range of monumental forms from which an architect can draw. Contemporary local claims that Olympia's was the fourth highest dome in the world may be exaggerated, but its dimensions surely place it in the upper ranks of that rarified breed. And its credentials as one of the last great self-supporting masonry domes can justifiably be cited; most domes in this country and abroad have exterior metal or masonry shells supported by some system of internal structural metal framing. Wilder and White were not modest in their ambitions for the Legislative Building nor intimidated by the spectacular technical problems that they and the builders would be facing in translating their plans into reality.

What they proposed was to build not one dome but three, meshing them into a structure soaring 176 feet above a base that was itself 102 feet above the ground, for an overall height of 278 feet. And all this by architects whose previous experience had been in a modest range of residential and small institutional work. Their audacity was impressive, but their success and that of their co-workers was an awesome achievement.

The builders began dealing with this challenging technology from the beginning of Phase Two work, with the excavations and subsequent forms, steel placement, and concrete pours for the foundation footings. The whole 130-foot monolith foundation slab, like a huge squared-off cushion, had been designed and placed to ensure that the tremendous loads of the dome and its piers could be transferred to bearing soil with no risk of later unequal settlement. On this footing rose the dome's four supporting corner piers, mammoth in their own right. The four-foot-thick reinforced-concrete walls of each pier formed a right angle whose sides were each 19′7″ long, and whose hypotenuse faced into the centerpoint of the rotunda. Vents, stairs, and elevator shafts were placed in the open centers of the piers.

*Progress photograph of construction,
May 19, 1924*

*Progress photograph of construction,
December 23, 1924*

Progress photograph of construction, March 28, 1925

Stonecutting for the Legislative Building at Walker Cut Stone Company, Tacoma, Washington

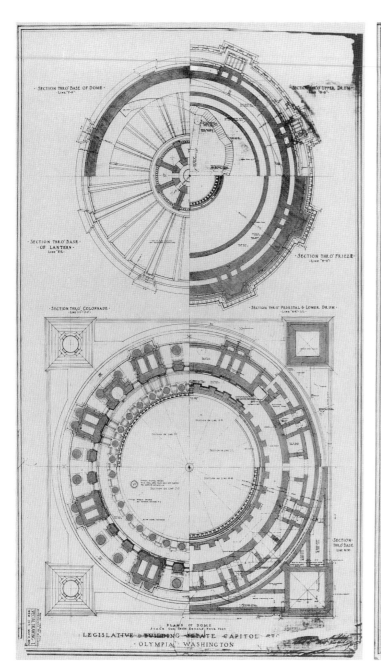

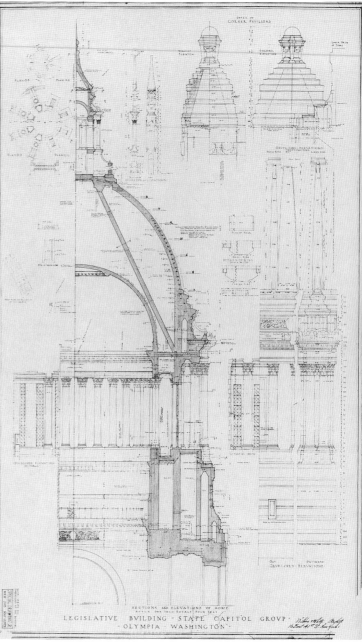

Construction drawings for the dome, 1925

Construction of the piers was not a particularly demanding task until the arches were reached. These would not only span from pier to pier, but their doubly curved intermediate surfaces, the pendentives, would also transpose the square plan of the rotunda and its approaching stairs into the circle of the dome's drum. This was a modern-day application of the principle of the pendentive dome, which the Byzantines had contributed to the repertoire of construction technology, dramatically demonstrated in Constantinople's sixth-century Hagia Sophia. All the weight of the dome is transferred down through the drum, the arches, and the pendentives into the four supporting piers. As in the construction of the pier footings, this was another crucial moment calling for intricate formworks and bracing, placement of webs of reinforcing steel, and a continuous concrete pour. This time, though, the pour had to take place a hundred feet above the building's surrounding terrace.

Phase Two ended with the completion of these arches and the square base from which the dome would rise. Initial Phase Three work, on the dome itself, was again one of those straightforward periods in construction that build toward complexity and tension. The ring of the drum was built up about 33 feet above the level of the square base to establish the baseline of the exterior 31-foot Corinthian colonnade and buttresses. By the end of 1925 a new height almost 70 feet above the Phase Two starting base had been established with the pouring of a continuous 16-foot-wide and 18-inch-deep reinforced concrete ring which set the structural level for the three domes.

The innermost dome, almost 60 feet in diameter and semicircular in section, is the one the visitor sees when standing on the rotunda floor 174 feet* below its apex (see page 81). Its drum is supported by an interior row of twenty-four 25-foot-high columns. These were to have been marble, but for economy the decision was made to stop the marble work in the rotunda at the springline of the arches, and the columns, together with all the other interior finish work above that line, were done in plaster instead. Their solid plaster encases steel columns.[10]

*Originally thought to have been 165 feet; recent measurements established this corrected figure.

The middle dome is conical; originally planned for brick masonry, this was later changed to a structural steel frame and intermediate reinforced-concrete panels. It has a maximum outside diameter of nearly 78 feet and is capped with a disk-shaped concrete slab designed to link with the top line of the outer dome. The slab's primary role, however, is to act as the foundation for the 31-foot-diameter lantern (the dome's uppermost ornamental cupola), and transfer its weight to the cone below. Those loads thus bypass the outer dome entirely, relieving it of any structural task except to support itself.

Nevertheless, the 80-foot-diameter outer dome is by far the most complex of the three. Its structure begins on the same concrete ring as the other domes, but its springline is about seventeen feet above that line, being built up to that level by brick bearing walls. By mid-May of 1926 the masons began building the dome's shell of brick and its exterior facing of stone upward and inward.

The construction of a masonry dome calls for challenging techniques, involving as it does doubly curved stone cuts, an absence of right angles, constant variations in dimensions, and in this case, some 1,400 stones, each requiring individual attention.

After the setting drawings are made, the plans go to the pattern floor [at the Walter Cut Stone Company]. In this room one fourth of the dome was laid out in full size. Every course from the bottom to the top is lined off on the floor and patterns taken from them on sheet zinc. This method detects any errors on the plans before they reach the cutting shop. . . .

A special machine was designed and built by the Walter Cut Stone Company to plane these stones in one operation. Each stone was placed on this machine in the exact position it would occupy in the finished dome. The cutting tools then cut the top and bottom beds and the face. All the roof stones are dovetailed together in such a way that the upper inside edge is above the lower outside edge of the next course above, similar to the way shingles are laid on a roof. This precludes the possibility of water leaking through the joints.[11]

Progress photograph of dome construction, May 18, 1926

Progress photograph of dome construction, October 13, 1926

Each carefully coded stone had its place within the structure; there it was accurately set by masons who were also alert to the problem of maintaining the dome's constant circle of course above course as they moved upward and inward toward the center. These techniques were splendidly successful.

One structural element that contributes to the dome's stability is nowhere visible. Unit construction like that of a masonry dome runs the risk of bursting outward from the weight of its materials. Wilder and White prevented this from happening by employing a number of design features: depth of wall section at the drum, buttresses, rib construction of the dome itself, and a system of bronze cables or ties that were grouted in between the dome's brick inner and stone outer shells in twenty-one successive levels, beginning at the springline and ending some twenty feet short of the final coursing of the stone outer shell.

White wrote to Johnston that Gunvald Aus, the firm's engineering consultant, was inquiring as to how the contractors had placed the cables, and Johnston answered:

As you may know the bronze cable was delivered in reels of from five to six thousand feet and instead of making numerous splices we hoisted the cable drum to the platform from which we were working and rolled the same around the circle the specified number of wraps. After this was done we clamped the two ends and used concrete blocks 1 inch square between the cable and the brick work so that when we were finished the cable was approximately 1 inch in the clear from the brick cone and having a uniform tension of each cable due to the fact that the several strands could come and go in the tightening process on account of having clamps only at the two ends.

I would not attempt to state what amount of tension we obtained but I do know that by striking the cables after the tightening process they would vibrate similar to a tightly drawn cable which in my mind shows that we have a tremendous tension.[12]

(Given present-day testing and code requirements, Johnston's methods seem charmingly archaic.)

By June 25 Johnston could report to the partners that the masons were at "т" course on the dome, about two-thirds up the sides of the shell. And the topmost course (course "dd" or the last of twenty-nine in all) was soon to key in with the slab disk of the middle dome, as they had each been designed to do.

Both this slab and the dome were so accurately placed that when the last course of stones on the dome were set there was just ½ inch clearance between them and the slab.

This space permitted the lining of both the concrete slab and the top course of stone with heavy sheet lead, thoroughly greased, and leaves the outer dome free to expand and contract under varying weather conditions. As a result of absolute precision maintained these changes in the outer dome will take place without affecting the lantern, which has ample clearance to be out of reach of the other surface, regardless [of] changes in conditions.[13]

The partners were still working on the final drawings for the lantern in April, but they finished in time for that work to remain on schedule. It added another 47 feet to the height of the Legislative Building, which topped out at 176 feet above Phase Two's square base and 278 feet above the building's terrace. The final stone on the lantern was set in place on October 13, 1926.*

In the meantime, another aspect of the stonework had been moving ahead: the ornamental carving. Most of this work, except for that on the dome, was done after the stone was in place. Thus, for example, the column capitals of the north and south porticoes, were put in position in a blocked-out raw state, and the stone carvers came in afterward to shape them into finished form.

The design for that form had been established by Wilder and White, but their drawings had then to be reinterpreted in full-scale plaster models. This work was done in New York by an "architectural sculptor" of that city, Maxfield H. Keck. His first contract (undated but presumably mid-1925) stipulated that he was to supply plaster "models for all ornamental stone, marble and plaster work and all bronze work, exclusive of the six main entrance doors."[14] The six doors were covered by a later contract. Ultimately, Keck was paid $21,655, including $5,000 for the doors.[15]

*There was intermittent attention given by the committee to the idea of adding an aircraft beacon to the dome, but nothing came of it.

Topping-out ceremonies for the Legislative Building,
October 13, 1926. Governor Hartley is the figure waving.
Jay Johnston is in the lower left-hand corner, wearing a cap.

The dome shortly after completion

Sculptor's studio mockup in plaster of Corinthian column and coffer ceiling for the Legislative Building portico

Carving in progress on south portico. Note the plaster-cast model at left and the partially completed capital at right.

Stone carvers at work on Corinthian columns for the portico. They are working from the plaster model at left.

Even in the 1920s it was hard to find men to do specialized work like stone carving. Initially the intention had been to subcontract the work; bids were received from only three firms, ranging from $160,462 to $167,250. Wilder and White were doubtful about the qualifications of all three but gave reluctant approval to one of the two low bidders (only $150 separated them). The Capitol Committee, however, preferred instead that Sound Construction do the work on a cost-plus-ten-percent basis "not to exceed $180,000." After an exchange of wires and letters the architects and the committee agreed on this arrangement, again without much enthusiasm from the architects, who wired the committee on September 28, 1925:

WE ARE ENTIRELY AGREEABLE TO AWARD OF CARVING TO SCCO ON COST PLUS BASIS IF COMMITTEE IS SATISFIED THIS IS TO BEST INTEREST OF THE STATE STOP WE PERSONALLY DOUBT WHETHER COMPETENT MASTER CARVER CAN BE OBTAINED AND DAMAGE DONE BY INCOMPETENT MEN TO STONE IN PLACE WILL BE IRREPARABLE

The committee replied that it was satisfied that Sound Construction would do the job in a manner satisfactory to the architects.

Finding a crew was another problem; Sound Construction was paid transportation costs for its personnel in their search for appropriately skilled labor. John Bruce, at the time working in California, was hired to be in charge of the carving work. He had been identified with nationally known work including "Biltmore" (the Vanderbilt residence in Ashville, N.C.), the U.S. Post Office in Seattle, and the Palace Hotel, the Civic Auditorium, and some large residences in San Francisco.[16]

The men who were assembled were drawn from all over the country and also included a number of Scotsmen with considerable stone-carving experience, mostly from the shires of Inverness and Ross. Alexander Munro* was one of those from Inverness; like the others he had already immigrated to this country to ply his trade before coming to Olympia. The project was fortunate to benefit from his talents, as he was in his sixties by that time and close to retirement.[17]

The work itself was done with a combination of hand tools and sandblasting equipment, the bulk of which the state purchased and later sold when the project was completed.† An undated and unidentified news clipping whose content places it sometime in the mid-1920s notes that

the stone carvers, artists wielding pneumatic chisels instead of pencil or brush, are busy making the capitals of the majestic columns of the entrance ways [based on] designs contemplated by the architect.

The Corinthian capitals for the 32 columns gracing the lower part of the dome, the capitals of pilasters and other ornamental work of the dome, were carved upon the ground before the blocks were hoisted to the dome proper. The great columns at the portico of the front or north entrance and for the porte cochere of the south entrance were placed, however, long before the carvers were on the job, so the capitals of these have to be carved from high scaffolding, and the work is now in progress. The carving of the cheneau, the ornamental stone coping running entirely around the building at the roof, is nearly completed and, it may be said that the bulk of the stone carving has been done.

*He was the grandfather of Ralph Munro, Washington's present secretary of state who is himself an admirer of the Legislative Building and an activist in its interests.

†The sale included a blacksmith's vise, cutting chisels, anvils, an electric grinder, an air hose, stone tools, a compressor, an electric motor, an air receiver, an endless belt, valves, gaskets, electric blowers, blast gates, chisel-tooth cutting machines, pipes and fittings, and tarps.

Cheneau detail

Skull and swag band course at the square base of the dome

Johnston also reported on the progress of the stone carving in a letter to the architects dated July 20, 1926:

The carving is progressing. The majority of the north portico columns are completed and I would say a couple of weeks more of the north front will about finish same. Figure on starting on the "Band Course at the Square Base of the Dome" the latter part of this week. I understand that Walker is getting out the column caps for the lantern in order that some may be carved before erection if possible.

There is no evidence that the architects ever regretted the carving contract going to Sound Construction; nor do observers today find any cause to do so.

There was one substantial area of work still to be completed: the placement of the ornamental metalwork, especially the major (Class A) light fixtures and the six entrance doors under the north portico. The most important light fixtures were those in the north portico and the south porte cochere, in the "monumental rooms" (e.g., the legislative chambers and the state reception room), and especially the one to hang in the rotunda. On the advice of the architects, the contract for light fixtures was let to the Tiffany Studios of New York City.[18] Louis Comfort Tiffany had established his company's reputation as a leader in American decorative arts at the turn of the century, and although remembered today mostly for its glassworks, it also produced many other objects including light fixtures and furniture. The Legislative Building's fixtures were all designed by Carl Moser. The state paid the company $158,000 for the contracted pieces.

The bronze rotunda chandelier, 8 feet in diameter and 25 feet high, was the major purchase. It was cast in Brooklyn, weighs 10,000 pounds, and cost the state exactly one dollar per pound. Suspended by a chain 101 feet long from the center of the inner dome, it hangs above the center point of the rotunda.* Directly beneath the chandelier, embedded in the floor of the rotunda, is a bronze seal of the the State of Washington, four feet in diameter, designed by Maxfield Keck.

*It must have been hung sometime before September 24, 1928, as the committee minutes of that date record a discussion about the $120.06 charge which the general contractors submitted for its hanging.

The items which most interested and preoccupied the committee and the architects were the six bronze entrance doors. They were to be a frequent subject of committee minutes and correspondence for over two years. They were more than doors, that was the problem. Their panels were to show future generations something of the state's past—but what?

The doors are first mentioned in committee minutes in February 1925, when a letter from the partners referred to them as a separate bidding item. On August 27 of that year they wrote the committee thanking it for approving the award of the modeling contract to Keck but continuing:

Except for the sculptural groups ultimately to be placed in front of the Temple of Justice, on the terrace pedestals at the Legislative Building, and as may be desired in the form of monuments at different places in the grounds, and the future sculpture in the pediments of the Legislative Building and the Insurance Building, there is no place so suited to interesting historical incidents as the panels of these bronze doorways. Naturally the modeling of such subjects involving as it would a degree of portraiture and sympathetic interpretations of incidents connected with the history of the State of Washington, would require capacity of the highest standing, and the cost of his services would be very considerably greater than the amount allowed.

We have therefore left out of our order to Mr. Keck, the modeling for these entrance doors, and if agreeable to you, we will postpone further suggestions until we have received the estimates for the stone carving. If as we hope, these latter estimates will run materially lower than our allowance, the balance can be used in connection with the bronze doors without exceeding the total cost of the building, [and] our allowance of $5,000 will give an entirely satisfactory result.

The bronze chandelier during installation

Wilder wrote separately to Savidge, the committee secretary, on December 4 regarding the doors:

The Great Seal embedded in the rotunda floor immediately beneath the dome

As we wrote you under date of August 27th, these doors are susceptible to either conventional or sculptural treatment, and we had thought that the saving on the stone carving might permit the latter. Upon further study, we have come to the conclusion that in any case the sculpture should be confined to the six main panels, which will materially reduce the cost.

On April 9, 1926, the Committee approved a separate $5,000 contract with Keck and asked Wilder and White to have him proceed with the work. However, Johnston wrote the partners the next day expressing some uneasiness:

The governor [Hartley], however, brought up the question in the Capitol Committee meeting yesterday of who was to pick out the subjects of those doors and I told him that the panels would be symbolic of Washington industries as per [our previous agreement]. This, however, did not seem to satisfy him and I believe it would be wise to get the Committee's approval on whatever subjects you intend to symbolize so that there will be no chance for an argument in the future.

The exchange continued across the country and in Olympia as to subject, relative costs (human figures cost more to model), and the absence of any major historical events in Washington's past. Wilder reminded the committee that this same dilemma had occurred in the choice of subject matter for some bronze work on the Insurance Building, and therefore the main industries of the state were used there: logging, shipping, and fisheries.[19] The committee decided early in June that it should collect appropriate photographs of early Washington scenes if it was to opt for the same solution on the Legislative Building. In a letter to the state's photographers (including Asahel Curtis, whose studio was in Seattle in the Colman Building) they explained that the committee was "anxious to secure some pictures of such scenes to forward to the architects, from which they may produce drawings for the models for casing the doors."[20] And the same day Johnston reported to Wilder and White that

a motion was carried to notify you to proceed with making preliminary drawings of the Front Entrance doors using subjects which are to be forwarded to Olympia for approval. I would suggest that these drawings be made up showing several variations of the subject so that they will have an opportunity of making a selection.[21]

But confusion and uncertainty persisted as to who was responsible for what. Wilder met with the committee in October, but it was still unable to come to a decision; the committee finally chose to abandon the effort and assign it to the architects. Perhaps in wry triumph, Wilder wired White on October 27 that

COMMITTEE FINALLY LEFT BRONZE ENTRANCE DOOR DESIGNS TO US APPROVING LUMBERING FISHERIES AND FARMING AS SUBJECT STOP FORWARDING PHOTOGRAPHS OF FIRST STEAM BOAT ORIGINAL CAPITOL BUILDING AND LOG CABIN FOR POSSIBLE BACKGROUND FEATURES BUT KECK CAN START MODELS

By March 1927, Wilder was able to present suggested designs for the doors—seven in all, for safe measure—and the committee chose five, asking for "an additional design showing the picture of an ox team." Two months later, though, it was still anxious about the doors. Johnston wrote the partners on May 2 that he was sending them some more photographs of ox teams (used to drag logs in the forest) which the committee had examined. He added that of Wilder's seven designs

No. 1 was most favorably acted upon by the Committee and in the discussion I stated that I was certain that the trees in the background could be extended in order to show the full tree in the panel itself. In No. 2 you will notice the old style method of fall where the fallers are up on the platform, and the Committee felt this should be shown in the panel if possible. We are forwarding the rest of the photos so that the modeler can use any part of them he might deem advisable. As soon as the model is complete the Committee desires cut of same be forwarded for approval. You will also receive in a day or two, I expect, copies [of the picture] showing the large trees which Mr. Wilder will recall hangs in the governor's office and which he thought might be of value in designing of the ox team panel. The Governor expects these at any time and has promised to let me know as soon as they arrive.

In May, Carl F. Gould, Bebb's partner, attended a meeting of the committee, and the subject of discussion again swung back to the doors:

Photographs were distributed and the Governor expressed his idea that the trees in the background should be somewhat larger than depicted in the photographs and that the log being drawn by the oxen appeared more prominent perhaps although he did not wish to hamper the sculptor's style by being too specific.[22]

But the models were finally revised to the committee's satisfaction, Keck was paid, the doors were cast by the William H. Jackson company in Brooklyn, and by the end of 1927 each of the two-thousand-pound doors had been shipped west and hung in place. (Ironically, most decisions affecting the progress of the construction of the building had been more fundamental to its success and therefore caused the committee hardly any pause at all!) And so, with the hanging of the north entrance doors, the Legislative Building took on much the same exterior appearance that it has today.

Bronze doors, north portico. Jay Johnston is on the left; the other man is unidentified. The ox-team design at the far right had particularly troubled the committee.

VI. Wrapping It Up

The final years of the project were mostly spent on interior work. During much of 1925 and 1926 the correspondence between the architects, the committee, and Johnston focused increasingly on decisions affecting the interior finishing, and particularly on the marble. Marble, befitting a building as monumental as this one, was the primary finish for all major and many minor public spaces: vestibules, stair halls, corridors, the rotunda, the Senate and House chambers, and the state reception room. The $850,000 contract for the marble had been awarded in mid-1925 to the Vermont Marble Company, with principal responsibility coming through its Tacoma plant; its quarries at Tokeen and Prince of Wales Island in Alaska were major sources. The cutting and polishing were done at the Tacoma works, the pieces then trucked to the site for setting. As with the stone carvers, a national search had to be conducted for marble setters, another specialized skill not available locally.

The partners were explicit in their instructions as to the setting of the marble, for sensitivity to its tonal values and pattern would do much to increase its effectiveness:

In placing the marble, please be guided by the following general rules. The darker and more heavily figured pieces are to be used nearest to the floor, and in the flat narrow bands rather than in the larger panels. The latter are to be matched on the vertical joint, but very prominent markings are to be avoided as the attention should be carried higher to the ornamented entablature above. . . . As a further general consideration, the lighter less figured pieces should be used at projecting portions and the dark heavily figured marble used in recesses. The monolithic columns in the State Reception Room will, of course require the most careful selection, for while on the above reason they should be comparatively light in tone, it may be difficult to avoid strongly featured marking which will give a very spotty effect. We should therefore prefer to have them all heavily marked or all comparatively light than to have part light and part dark.[1]

The light gray tones of Alaskan marble were featured in most of the monumental spaces: entrances, stairs, corridors, and especially the rotunda. Richer and more colorful (and more expensive) imported marble was used in the legislative chambers and in the state reception room.

The rotunda, located directly beneath the dome, is not only the main axial feature around which the chief functions of the building are keyed, it also provides an enormously effective, monumental spatial experience. There had been a move by the committee to use all marble rather than using plaster above the entablature of the marble veneer, where it stopped at the springline of the arches of the piers. The committee's resolution of December 14, 1925, asking the legislature to authorize the necessary additional funding had been unanimously carried. The legislature, however, was cool to the idea and later the governor was, too, though he had originally supported it. It appears that more marble was aesthetically advisable, but politically clumsy. The governor wrote to the other members of the committee:

It is my opinion that the placing of marble for the entire height of the rotunda would only serve to lend a ghastly cold air to an otherwise beautiful building. . . .

Also, I have made it a point to find out what the people think of it and they feel the legislators at the legislature did the right thing in turning it down and if they did pass it, I would veto it. I understand the situation fully now.[2]

Interior view of the rotunda, shortly after completion

View from the rotunda into the dome, 1985

The interior finish of the dome, therefore, remained plaster. The plasterwork throughout the building totals some 54,000 square yards. Much of it is richly ornamented, for example, on the Corinthian capitals of the dome and the ceilings in the Senate and House and in the state reception room. The designs were Keck's; his models were shipped to Olympia for the plasterers to work from.

Into the marble stair landing directly under the dome was set Keck's cast bronze Great Seal of the State of Washington, featuring a portrait of George Washington encircled by oak leaves. Its placement was immediately controversial—various patriotic organizations objected to the location as insufficiently respectful of the Father of the Country.

The Washington State Society of the Sons of the American Revolution, at a special meeting decided to use every lawful means to have removed from the floor of the Capitol at Olympia the cast of the face of George Washington.

We are not at this time concerned with who was responsible for this outrage but it is our intention to locate and hold up for public ridicule the person or persons who are responsible for its continuation.[3]

The rotunda floor with the Great Seal beneath the dome, the state reception room and south entrance beyond

The Senate chamber

Similar protests were received by the committee from the Ladies of the Grand Army of the Republic (Seattle), the United Spanish American War Veterans (Spokane), the Seattle Board of the Daughters of the American Revolution, and the Seattle Federation of Women's Clubs.

The governor wrote to the DAR on August 4, 1928, that he presumed

the architect, in placing this bronze medallion . . . at the center of the east and west and north and south axis of the building and the most conspicuous place, did so for the reason that it would be seen by more people than in any other possible location. Have no brief to speak for him, but do not believe he intended any disrespect or indignity. Perhaps he figures that the public could show its patriotism and respect by not walking on the plaque.

Johnston also mentioned the criticism, writing to Wilder on September 25 that

The Governor for once was with us and stated he thought you had picked an appropriate place and that people ought to have enough respect not to walk over same. He was very much against any kind of enclosure and would be in favor of removing it altogether rather than have a barrier of any kind around it.

People did walk on it, however, respectful or not. Even as late as 1929 the seal's location continued to be a source of concern. "George Washington's nose is already badly worn off by the reason, apparently, of thousands having walked over his face."[4] Finally, in the late 1930s, Governor Hartley long since departed, the roped enclosure was installed that is found there today.

Additional bronze work completed the rotunda. The fourth floor balcony railings incorporate replicas of the state seal. And at each corner of the rotunda are replicas of Roman firepots used for indirect lighting. Designed by Keck, they were cast in the Brooklyn foundaries of the William H. Jackson Company, which had furnished the bronze work for the Temple of Justice.

The Senate and House chambers and the state reception room were all finished in imported and more colorful marble. For the Senate, Wilder chose Rose Fomosa marble from Germany with (as he described it) rose-colored clouding, though in a letter of September 1, 1925, to the marble company, he asked that there be "no deep red spots that exceed 1 inch wide." The result was darker than either the architect or the Senate members would have liked; nevertheless, the effect is handsomely rich with graded tones from almost black to pearl gray and veins of rose and yellow. In the House the marble is French Escalette, which gives this chamber a lighter and warmer tone with its basic ground of cream and cloudings and veins of yellow, pink, and red.

Of the state reception room, Wilder wrote to the marble company that it "is intended to be the most ornate in the building and a degree of figure and color in the marble is to be desired."[5] He chose Bresche Violet marble from Italy, also with a cream background but with veining of red, lavender, and green that results in greater contrast and considerable liveliness. The fireplaces, one in each end wall, were designed for burning wood or coal, but the architect advised against their use because smoke could discolor the dome. The chimneys therefore were blocked off and electric grates installed. The room was finished with teak floors and two Czechoslovakian crystal chandeliers supplied by Tiffany's.

Bronze Roman firepot, one of four in the rotunda

The state reception room

In July 1926, the committee began to examine the question of furnishings for the Legislative Building. It was no incidental matter, for the monumental character of the building required appropriate furniture to avoid any cheapening of the architectural effects, the full potential of which was clearly emerging. Even the legislators seemed moved by what was being created, for their authorization of $600,000 to cover furnishing costs was reasonably generous and had no conditions except that the committee and the architects "spend the money as judgment dictated." The committee (with the encouragement of the architects) decided that custom designs and construction were required rather than selections out of a catalogue. As had been done with the light fixtures, the furnishings (including furniture, window and wall hangings, draperies, and rugs) were divided into five different groups depending on the status of their assigned location. Class A furniture (divided into three subgroups) was for such ceremonial spaces as the Senate and House chambers, the state reception room, and executive offices, and received the greatest attention in its selection.

The partners were very much involved in that selection, anxious that the results not dull the impact of their monument. They had recommended to the committee the specifications for bidding, and these were approved in early August, followed shortly by a national announcement of a call for bids.

All bidders were asked to keep in mind the kind of building for which the designs were being sought and to make their own suggestions to ensure compatibility. On September 30, 1926, the awards were made, the Class A contract going to W. and J. Sloane of New York City. The total bids came to $510,000, which was $90,000 less than the authorization.[6]

The architects themselves designed the desks for the two legislative chambers, after consultation with their leaders and members. The Senate desks were of mahogany, the House desks of walnut, their colors coordinated to their location.

The furnishings in the state reception room were (appropriately) more ceremonial, especially an enormous seven-foot-diameter table in the middle of the room. The rug was specially woven (in a rather unprepossessing design) and seamless. Heavy lined velvet drapes with matching valences and silk cable tasseled ties completed what has been called the state's "parlor."

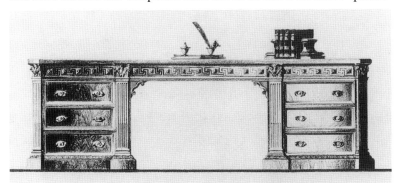

Governor's eight-foot desk ($900)

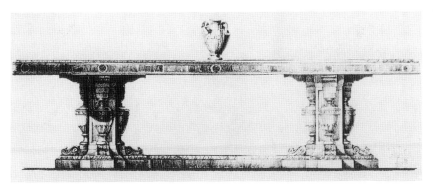

Ten-foot table for governor's office ($975)

Seven-foot round table for state reception room ($1,000)

W. & J. Sloane design sketches for furnishings

Governor's desk chair ($250)

Swivel chairs for Senate and House

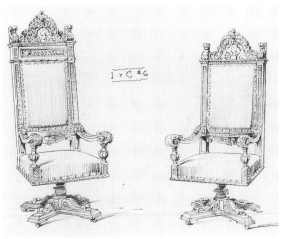

Senate and House speaker's stand

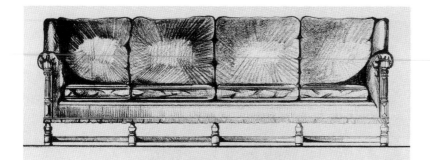

W. & J. Sloane design sketches for furnishings

Nine-foot davenport for cabinet room ($700)

Bookcase ($1,150), the most expensive item on the Class A-1 listing

Clerk's desk for the Senate and House

One aspect of the interior finishing which the plans for the Legislative Building specified but which was never implemented was its "mural paintings." Walls in the rotunda, the south stair hall, the Senate and House, and the state reception room were identified for that treatment, but they remain today almost as bare as they were over fifty years ago. Perhaps, after the trauma of dealing with the six relatively small panels on the bronze entrance doors, the prospect of facing similar frustrations blown up to the dimensions of mural paintings was too intimidating for either the committee or the architects to face at that late date in the project's history. If there was any serious move in the 1920s to push for them, the records are silent on the subject. It may be that the economic climate of the 1930s simply precluded such a use of funds. (Since then there have been twelve different efforts to fulfill the intentions of the building's designers. For various reasons—costs, selection of artist, subject matter, aesthetics—all have been frustrated. In the

The governor's office

late 1970s, with an increased interest in and appreciation of the building, leaders in both the legislative and executive branches of state government made yet another effort toward completion of the murals. Selection of the artists was by a committee chosen from the arts community, and the choice of two painters and the subsequent installation of murals on several walls in the Senate and House Chambers seemed remarkably promising. But the abstract character of the designs, and especially the interpretation of "obscenity" that some viewers made of what they saw, caused enough outcry not only to stop the project but, in the case of the House Chamber, to require the curtaining off of the murals. Thus the interest, richness, and color that the designers had originally envisioned for the building has been postponed once again.)

Finally, there was the matter of landscaping. Since the original 1911 competition the campus had been extended between Eleventh and Fourteenth Streets eastward to Capitol Way, an area that had been occupied at one time or another by the pioneer home of the state's first territorial governor, the high school, the local hospital, and some modest but substantial residences. Needed now was a plan for incorporating this added space and the grounds immediately surrounding the group into a unified landscape scheme. Surprisingly—considering the history of relations between Olmsted Brothers and the commission—the firm was again approached to develop a landscape plan for the now expanded capitol campus. According to a letter written by Wilder and White to the Olmsteds, dated July 7, 1927, the architects had assured the committee that if it would employ "some firm like the Olmsted Brothers [for advice on] the general treatment of the grounds, the highest results will be achieved, and we will cooperate in every way." An agreement had been reached, and the architects were bringing the landscape architects up to date.

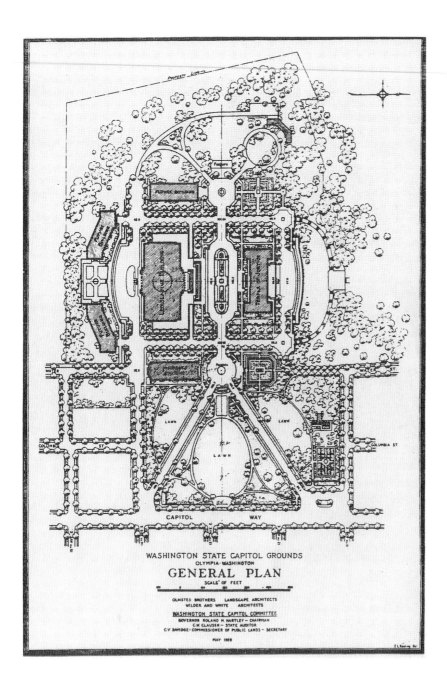

WASHINGTON STATE CAPITOL GROUNDS
OLYMPIA-WASHINGTON
GENERAL PLAN
SCALE OF FEET

OLMSTED BROTHERS LANDSCAPE ARCHITECTS
WILDER AND WHITE ARCHITECTS

WASHINGTON STATE CAPITOL COMMITTEE
GOVERNOR ROLAND H. HARTLEY — CHAIRMAN
C.W. CLAUSEN — STATE AUDITOR
C.V. SAVIDGE — COMMISSIONER OF PUBLIC LANDS — SECRETARY

MAY 1928

In doing so, they reflected once more on the origins of their group plan and the rationale for its configurations:

The Olmsted Brothers' plan for the Capitol campus, 1928

It may be well at this time to outline our conception of the Group, so that you may understand the purpose of certain features. As you know, this Group is made up of a series of small units, which in the more usual conditions are combined to make a single unit of sufficient magnitude to have great dignity on that score alone. Our early studies in the original competition in 1911, convinced us that only by so arranging the subordinate buildings as to screen the substructure of the Legislative Building, could a broad enough base be provided for a dome of proper size, and this not only accounts for the location of the Temple of Justice directly in front of the Legislative Building, but also prevents the full value of the Group being obtained until the three additional subordinate buildings are erected to the south and west of the Legislative Building.

As we have seen, this scheme for proportioning the dome to the group of buildings as a whole evolved out of restudies that the architects carried out in the 1920s. The rationale in Wilder and White's letter reinforces their design approach, and they may have had it in mind in 1911. But they did not put forward this defense at the time, and it may, indeed, be a convenient after-the-fact explanation for the realities which the Olmsteds were now being asked to face.

In the resulting general plan, which the Olmsteds completed in May 1928, the axial approach from the north was entirely abandoned (except in the visual lines), the victim of both changing tastes and a more realistic estimate of the cost it would involve. Thus, the landscape architects needed to develop a scheme that would integrate the north-south axis of the group plan with connections eastward to Capitol Way and the city. They chose to do so by honoring the secondary east-west axis that moves symmetrically between the Legislative Building and the Temple of Justice. Rather than continuing that line directly east to Capitol Way, however, they proposed a roundpoint at the north front of the Insurance Building, from which two diagonals connected to Capitol Way, one to the southeast and one to the northeast leading to the central city. It was a compromise at best, vaguely reminiscent of the diagonal that they had included in their 1912 plan between the group and downtown. Like the earlier plan, this one could not overcome the awkwardness of an approach from the east to an ensemble oriented to the north. One arrives at the Court of Honor between the Legislative Building and the Temple of Justice by sidling across the campus at an angle that fails to offer the axial and sequential monumentality appropriate to the concept.

Great lawned areas inside and outside of the diagonals were laid out with curving walks that connected with sweeping lines to the other parts of the campus. The axis and sight lines to the Capitol group and especially to the dome from Capitol Way were thereby preserved but in a rather informal way, with clustered groupings of trees and many irregular beds of shrubbery bordering the walks. (In subsequent development of the grounds these beds were eliminated.)

In the areas closest to the tight symmetry of the existing buildings and those projected for the future, more planting formality was retained. There the trees were ranked in parallel rows along the streets and axes in suitable recognition of the planning spirit which had shaped the group plan. In two locations the plan indicated the geometrical beds of formal gardens, though only one, a sunken garden north of the Insurance Building, was ever installed. The other was planned in association with the old Governor Stevens house (presumed to have been the residence of the territory's first governor), northeast of the campus. Later both the frame house and the garden were removed from the plan and the house torn down. The site plan included no areas specifically designated for parking, which was presumably to be adequately served by some open plazas or at street curbs.

Wilder and White were asked to comment on the Olmsteds' proposal, and Wilder's response was mixed. As he explained in his letter to the committee of October 11, 1927,

In general, they have simply reversed the treatment of the grounds indicated on such plans as we have made, in the past. The essential idea in each was, so far as possible, to unite again into a single effect, six isolated buildings, no one of which could afford to stand alone. We proposed to accomplish this by closely planting the grounds outside the groups, leaving the space within the group as open as possible By using broad avenues and plazas and by restricted and very formal planting, the necessary contrast would be secured. On the other hand, they propose to plant the surrounding grounds very openly and the area within very closely, thus obtaining the same contrast but in different ways.

That same letter also refers to Wilder and White's plans in response to the property acquisitions east to Capitol Way. Unfortunately, the plans are no longer extant, but his description helps to establish the partners' approach in contrast to that of the Olmsteds:

Our plans contemplated a broad double avenue with central parking strip located on the axis of the main plaza. This would not only afford a very monumental approach, but from it one would obtain a view of the group far more magnificent than is possible from any other angle. At this point the future office building to the west will combine with the Legislative and Insurance Buildings to give the effect of a single building unsurpassed in size by even the National Capitol. . . .

The Olmsted plan contemplated two diagonal approaches. . . . It is argued that these diagonal approaches avoid a right angle turn from Capitol Way and that through that from 11th Street a vista of the dome will be obtained. Against them, we see the impossibility of treating them monumentally or of affording a satisfactory vista in the opposite direction; the awkward size and shape of the fore court where

Campus clearance and grading work, ca. 1929. Photograph by Vibert Jeffers, © 1985 by Susan Parish/First Light Media Collection, Olympia.

they meet, which is out of proportion to the other open spaces, [and] the danger of isolating the Legislative Building by the attempted vista of the dome. . . . In view of the above, we would suggest that Messrs. Olmsted Brothers be asked to give this matter further consideration and see if a satisfactory solution cannot be found for an approach on the axis of the main plaza.

Wilder's letter also expressed other concerns about the Olmsted proposals: the abandonment of waterfront improvements, the treatment of the plaza north of the Temple of Justice, the scale and location of gardens to the Temple's east and west, the "unfortunate" vulnerability of the plaza south of the Legislative Building to parking, the "impracticality" of Fifteenth Street as a service entrance, and the like. He closed by referring to a redrawing of their own plan (also missing from the records, so there is no way of knowing the extent to which the partners' suggestions affected the final Olmsted plan). In due course, however, the Olmsted plan received architectural and committee approval, and after clearance, grading, paving, and planting, it was mostly in place by 1930.

One issue of campus planning that remained to be decided was a piece of business postponed from the end of the First World War. The 1919 legislature had approved state funds for the erection of a monument honoring the soldiers, sailors, and marines of Washington who lost their lives in the war. The campus plan of that date, however, was still too uncertain to establish a location for the monument, and the matter was left in limbo. In 1928, however, Alonzo Lewis, the sculptor, presented a design to the committee, they approved it, and Lewis completed the sculpture. Now followed the question of a location; the roundabout north of the Insurance Building was being considered.

Lewis sent Wilder a photograph of the monument. Though agreeable to the monument itself, Wilder objected to the roundabout as a site. Ever loyal to strict formality, he pointed out that a monument there would call for a balancing monument in a similar roundabout shown on the Olmsted plan directly west across the campus. He also felt that the proposed location had the sculptured figures marching forward in a strong directional movement that failed to coordinate with campus axes. Wilder much preferred that the monument be located somewhere in the new easterly campus area, which had its own space and planting outside the immediate context of the Capitol group.

World War I monument, Alonzo Lewis, sculptor

Mr. Wilder appreciated that the committee has not asked his advice in this connection and understands further that Olmstead [sic] Brothers have approved the location. He has no desire to complicate the situation, but if the committee wishes, he will be glad to discuss the matter with Mr. Lewis and the Olmsted Brothers and see if another location would be less open to objection. Here again, no charge to the state would be involved.[7]

However, the committee preferred their original inclination, and in due course the monument was placed in the eastern roundabout, its figures marching off into the east across the Olmsted oval toward Capitol Way and (in those days) the relocated high school.

The capitol campus project was brought substantially to a close by the completion of landscaping. The Legislative Building was considered officially complete in 1928.* Contemporary reports gave the building's total cost as $6,791,595.88, the furnishings $594,172.33, for a grand total of $7,385,768.21. The 1980s equivalent of that sum would be about fifty-five million dollars— far less than such a project would cost today, even if technically possible.

*The legislature met there for ceremonial purposes in the last days of the 1927 session.

Various odds and ends in connection with such a complex and ambitious effort lingered on into 1929, but the tempo had slowed almost to a halt. Sound Construction personnel were back in Seattle, and Wilder had returned for the last time to New York; Johnston released his key to the state's business control director. The Capitol Committee remained on stage as the last principal performer of the construction effort with more than a sentimental attachment to the project for which so much had been dared and so much achieved. Nineteen twenty-nine saw the end of the Legislative Building as an active construction project, and the end of an exuberant and self-confident era in the economic history of state and nation.

VII. The Legislative Building's Design Lineage

No building is conceived in a vacuum and isolated from influences, and certainly not the Legislative Building with all its links to major themes in Western architectural history and contemporary precedents. Wilder and White, nurtured in that history by education and familiar with the precedents by professional experience, were the instruments by which the building was shaped, but to know the building that resulted requires further investigation into its design lineage. Important, too, is an awareness of the processes by which design decisions were arrived at and how the building thus evolved toward what the architects intended and the builders built. The disappearance of the partners' office records of their Olympia work makes the search more difficult, but there is nevertheless strong inferential evidence to work with.

As protégés of the firm of McKim, Mead and White, both Wilder and White had learned its lessons well. A major, perhaps foremost practitioner of the American Renaissance, the firm had been one of those brought to the 1893 Columbia Exposition to give that event the architectural image that was to so move its observers and shape standards of design practice for the next twenty years. Charles Follen McKim and Stanford White were the firm's star designers; William Rutherford Mead was the managerial support. Their forte was the successful use of models from classical Rome or the Roman Renaissance, eclectically adjusted and blended for the skillful satisfaction of current conditions: buildings handsome, assured, and infinitely gratifying to their many public and private clients. The Low Library at Columbia University (1894), a reuse of a classical Roman dome with Greek and Beaux Arts details; Pennsylvania Station (1906–1910), its lineage and spatial drama those of Rome's Baths of Caracalla; the University Club (1900) and the elegant little (in comparison) Pierpont Morgan Library (1902–1906), both evoking memories of the Italian Renaissance: all were in New York and all became familiar to Wilder and White in the years they worked and developed under the ægis of the office from whose drafting tables those designs had come.

Before coming to New York, both men had also been trained in schools of architecture that stressed the design approaches of the French École des Beaux Arts. White was a graduate of the first school in the United States founded specifically to prepare its graduates for careers in architecture, the Massachusetts Institute of Technology, whose curriculum was based on William Ware's study of the École's methods. MIT and Cornell, where Wilder studied, like most contemporary architectural schools subscribed to the fashion of appointing French École graduates as instructors and design critics, reinforcing the École example. The design standards represented by that example emphasized composition, symmetry, order, subordination, correctness of detail, and the primacy of classical and Renaissance precedent in the selection of inspiration for contemporary applications.

Before their partnership Wilder and White had also begun to visit Europe and see *in situ* the origins of their inspiration; White was to return there a number of times, especially to Italy, which he held in special affection. Thus, by training, experience, and inclination, the architects were prepared to carry on the the American Renaissance tradition—and to do so skillfully— after leaving McKim, Mead and White.

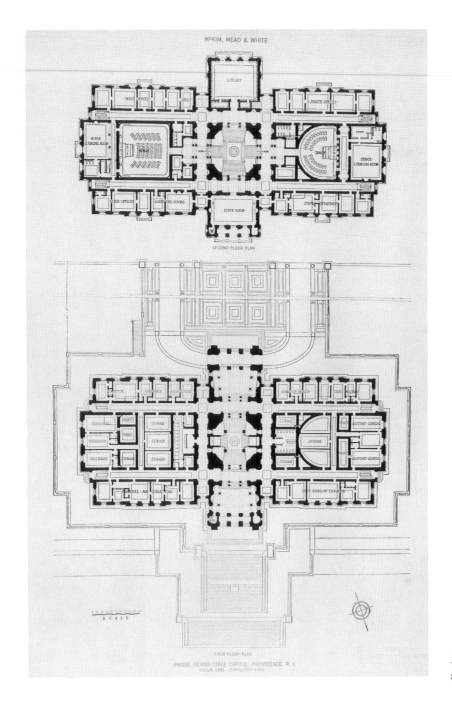

Rhode Island State Capitol first and second floor plans

Just as their mentors would have done, Wilder and White approached the design of the Legislative Building by combining elements from a number of sources. In doing so, they acknowledged their place in a lineage largely established in this country by the older firm. But like others who had been nurtured in the same experience, once they began practicing independently, though they may have retained their respect for the clarity of classicism and the Renaissance in general and McKim, Mead and White in particular, as a younger generation they sought interpretations less restrained, less academic, more full-bodied, richer, more vigorous. This may explain why architects for capitols such as those of Minnesota, Pennsylvania, Missouri, Mississippi, Wisconsin, Utah, and others[1] were all influenced in varying degrees by McKim, Mead and White but concluded with designs more sympathetic to the expansive new American twentieth century of which they were more immediately a part. The City Beautiful Movement was an appropriate reflection of their ambitions, and this newer generation of architects and their capitols were expressive of it.

McKim, Mead and White's work on the Rhode Island Capitol took place during 1891–1904; the project spanned most of the time Wilder and White spent with that firm. They may not have worked on it directly, but without question they were very much aware of it and would draw from it for their own chef d'oeuvre. Nor were they alone. As Leland Roth has noted, the Rhode Island Capitol "became a model for a generation of new capitol buildings across the country."[2]

The Rhode Island Capitol was a commission that came to the firm by a competition to which it had been specifically invited and which it won in January 1892. Mead had been the entry's principal author with a proposal notable for clarity in both plan and form. Comparing the plans with Wilder and White's construction drawings some thirty years later for Olympia (see pages 54 and 55), one can clearly see the debt owed to the earlier building. In both cases visitors ascend monumental exterior stairs on a north-south axis to an entry beyond which interior stairs continue to an intermediate landing in which the state seal is embedded in the floor directly beneath the dome. Thereafter, one turns to final flights of stairs on the east-west axis, leading to the legislative floor—the Senate to the east, the House to the west. Each building also has its state reception room facing south on that floor as well. The major difference in plans was that Rhode Island's principal entrance facade faced south whereas Olympia's was to the north. Interior views also suggest precedents set by the earlier building: the domed rotundas—though with important scale differences—and the remarkably similar reception rooms (compare pages 81 and 84 with the illustrations below).

Rhode Island State Capitol rotunda

Rhode Island State Capitol reception room

External similarities are weaker, a tendency that Wilder and White shared with other designers of their era. Thus, Rhode Island's dome is subdued, somewhat narrow, vertical, its parts composed in a manner acknowledging Wren at St. Paul's or Soufflot's Pantheon in Paris. In Olympia, however—like Cass Gilbert (Minnesota), Joseph Huston (Pennsylvania), or Tracy and Swartwout (Missouri)—though willing to learn from their mentors, Wilder and White's tastes ran toward something more robust, even French Baroque, in mannerisms. The Paris domes of the Mansarts come to mind: Val-de-Grace or the Invalides. Only the tourelles the partners added in 1920 suggest lingering external ties with Rhode Island, especially in the 1923 plans when they lost their pyramids and became domes (compare pages 56 and 103 with the illustrations below and opposite).

Rhode Island State Capitol

The break with Rhode Island precedent, however, is indicated in more than outward appearance. Wilder and White seem to have responded to an alternative influence that had already had an impact on the Rhode Island dome itself. This was Cass Gilbert's Minnesota State Capitol, which was under construction in 1898, ahead of Rhode Island's. The dimensions of the Rhode Island dome had been increased by five feet upon the discovery that Minnesota's dome was the larger.[3] Wilder and White's awareness of Gilbert's dome is evident structurally. The Minnesota model is a triple-dome construction, unlike the double dome at Rhode Island. Olympia's dome, as already seen, was based on a threesome of inner and outer shells with an internal structural cone supporting the lantern, exactly mirroring the structure in Minnesota (compare page 66 with the illustration at far right).

*The domes of the
Minnesota State Capitol, the
Pennsylvania State Capitol, and the
Missouri State Capitol*

The outer domes of all three capitols, however, had one common and prestigious trait: each was self-supporting masonry requiring no internal metal skeleton.

Unlike McKim, Mead and White, who designed their dome as the crowning feature for a single building, Wilder and White designed theirs as the dominant feature of a group of buildings. This may further account for the differences between the two domes, particularly in height, for here too there is a significant movement away from McKim, Mead and White toward a more independent treatment of the problem. Wilder and White left behind Rhode Island's attenuated model and developed a grander and more fulsome solution based on markedly different circumstances and tastes. Their initiative culminated in a partnership of group, building, and dome whose design success marked the architects' break with their past and coming of age.

This break with the Rhode Island precedent was demonstrated further in the partners' handling of the main body of the building with its colonnaded and pedimented porticoes and lateral wings. As already seen, they employed a more classical order, with ranks of Corinthian columns in the porticoes and smaller Doric columns supporting lateral entablatures and gabled roofs, expressing the bicameral nature of the building and handsomely flanking and visually reinforcing the base from which rises the dome.

There is a site feature of the Olympia Capitol and its Rhode Island cousin, however, which enhances their similarity. Both buildings rise above raised balustraded terraces, and the main entrances are therefore approached by grand staircases that have a dramatic impact on their occupants and on visitors. (Each was also to have had esplanaded extensions to a waterfront, but in neither case was this realized.[4] Rhode Island's Capitol at least avoided Olympia's folly; its view still lies unblocked before it.)

On the whole, Wilder and White's development of their Olympia project—so far as the existing record allows us to infer—evolved with notable serenity. Award of the commission was followed by minor site revisions but more particularly by detailed study for the Legislative Building (the competition had called only for the suggestion of its presence as part of the group plan). Thereafter, once the decision had been made to abandon the Flagg foundations, adjustments in certain alignments, proportions, and details might occur but the basic parti remained.

Dome section detail of the Minnesota State Capitol. From Minnesota's State Capitol: The Art and Politics of a Public Building, © *Minnesota Historical Society.*

The Legislative Building shortly after completion of the dome

Differences show up, however, between the drawings of 1912 and those of 1920 and 1923. The earlier view (see page 48) presented a building that was higher and more compact in its proportions, with a cornice line that maintained a constant elevation around the entire building, including its entrance porticoes. Neither of the legislative chambers had any significant external expression, so that, except for the dome, the building could have been taken for the architecturally pretentious housing of administrative offices. The differentiation between the Legislative Building and its surrounding support structures in the group came largely from its central location, an elevated position on its own terrace, and, of course, the dome. But the colonnaded facades, unity of cornice lines, and an unpretentious but dignified use of the classical design vocabulary were evident throughout the group.

The eight years' work in Olympia that followed those 1912 decisions brought the firm both increased professional experience and further opportunities for reflection on the central feature of the group plan. So, with work on the Temple of Justice and the Insurance Building either completed or progressing comfortably, when in 1920 the partners again turned their attention to the Legislative Building, it was not surprising that they would have second thoughts. The response was partly functional. Recognizing the number of offices requiring housing, an additional attic-level floor was tucked in rather effectively just above the continuous cornice line that horizontally girdled the building. The attic had its own cornice, its line enriched by sculpted cheneaux that tied in with the same treatment of the portico gables. The Doric order was used throughout, a reflection of its use on the Temple of Justice and the Insurance Building and of its relative economy.

More obvious, however, is the 1920 break with the somewhat Florentine Early Renaissance dome of 1912 and a return to the inspiration of Wilder and White's original competition drawings, the more mature Roman Renaissance, and particularly the dome of St. Peter's. The colonnade that supported the 1912 dome was retained, with its strong vertical pattern of lights and darks, but the drum is circular again, as is the dome, its surface marked with ribs and a single line of small lunettes. These and the obelisks that mark the springline of the dome and the module of its ribs gave the ensemble a somewhat florid interpretation.

The compactness of the main body of the building is emphasized, even exaggerated, by the oppressive height of the drum and dome. Though the vertical dimensions of the drum and dome were necessary if the dome was to be compositionally the central feature of the group, their impact on the Legislative Building made for an uncomfortable partnership. Fortunately, the subsequent abandonment of the Flagg foundations provided the architects with a new opportunity.

The elevational changes recorded in the 1923 drawings (see pages 56 and 57), which were almost all incorporated in the final design, are crucial, though at first glance they might even be missed. The nearly eighty feet of overall building length beyond the 1893 foundations provided a much more horizontal base on which to build, and in place of the boxlike compactness of the earlier proposals there was a succession of levels and setbacks toward a central square base or platform from which the dome would rise.

The four stories of 1920 remained, their functions contained in wings that kept the same subdued terrace-level floor supporting a two-story Doric colonnade and entablature. The attic level, however, was set back behind the wall line of the lower floors but with the same richly crested rhythm of cheneaux of 1920. And above, though well back from their line, rose the now gabled roofs of the two legislative chambers.

To a considerable extent these changes led to the success of the dome in its relationship with the Legislative Building and the group. Recognizing early that their dome was the dominant presence for a group of buildings rather than a single building, Wilder and White planned accordingly. At the same time they managed a harmony between dome and building which McKim, Mead and White failed to achieve at Rhode Island. With the latter, the base, tourelles, and dome are simply superimposed on a subservient building; their absence might be little missed. That would be impossible in Olympia where the whole Legislative Building was composed visually to fulfill its role as foundation for its dome. It was managed with remarkable panache, enhanced further when the partners wisely decided to discard the lingering and rather dated Rhode Island motif of the tourelles, substituting low-profiled corner pylons in their place that added further to the strength and harmony of the building's silhouette.

The terrace and monumental north approach staircase of the main entrance* remained in the 1923 plans but with certain differences in their relationship to the rest of the building. Instead of emerging almost directly from the east and west colonnades, as in 1920, the portico was given considerably more framing and mass. Part of the added building width was used to introduce solid masonry walls on either side of the portico, their planes stepping forward to frame it handsomely as well as adding a visually much more satisfying foundation for the platform and the sequential levels of the dome itself.

Thus the architects, as they moved further from their earlier experiences, used the opportunity to overcome the imbalances of their 1920 design. A much-improved central frontispiece of portico and supporting wall frames built outward and upward to establish a base for the dome. The subsidiary wings to the east and west provided similar reinforcement with successive planes and levels of setbacks, entablatures, and roofs. Solid in handling, restrained in detail, the design managed the enormous task of carrying the weight and richness of a dome scaled to satisfy the perceptual needs of the group plan. Together they would achieve a splendid compositional balance.

Within the format imposed by the mass of the building, the architects chose details which were strongly classical Roman, taking their cue from what had already been done for the Temple of Justice and the Insurance Building. The colonnades of both wings match those of the earlier buildings—unfluted Roman Doric. The functional design prominence of the entrance porticoes is given added accent by columns over thirty feet high, the capitals now changed to the Corinthian order closely following Rome's Pantheon, though somewhat simplified in the interests of economy and the techniques employed for their *in situ* carving. Important foils to the general restraint in the building's use of ornament are the handsome cheneaux that follow and richly accent the gables and cornice lines and the single skull and swag band course that is a belt around the platform supporting the dome (see page 74.)

A combination of design taste and economic restraints served the Legislative Building extremely well. Given the bulk of the building with its wall planes of stone, rusticated at the first floor but smooth above, the effectiveness of the detail where it occurs is considerable. What one sees today—save for the corner pylons, an accessory feature of the dome noted below—is without significant change from the drawings of 1923.

Carved ornament was, of course, vulnerable to economics, easily deleted in the face of costs. The Legislative Building had already been affected by this type of decision when the columnar treatment of the Temple of Justice had been switched from the original fluted and florid Corinthian order to the

The north and south porticoes are almost identical except that, for the latter, the terrace elevation is on grade, permitting it to be developed as a porte cochere.

Corinthian capital for a portico

much more restrained and less costly unfluted Doric columns. That decision would establish a similar design format for all subsequent units of the group plan.

The architects felt it necessary that the committee understand how, in this framework of restraint, ornament could add visual emphasis and richness that would be especially appropriate for the Legislative Building as the centerpiece of the group plan. Wilder explained this to the committee in early April 1923:

On the exterior we have maintained the same severe simplicity of the other buildings at the two wings, but at the main entrance portico and the corresponding cornice at either side as well as on the dome itself we have introduced a very considerable amount of carving. We feel that this building, representing as it does the center of the state's activities, deserves a richness of effect only to be obtained from decorated surfaces, and while this decoration could in some degrees be lessened, we trust that its expense will appeal to you as having justification.[5]

He was reasonably successful in his efforts. Except for the sculpture in the north and south portico pediments, a narrow and rather inconspicuous sculptured band around the drum of the dome, and the clock faces proposed for the north and south elevations just above the dome platform, the architects' wishes for the building's surface detail were honored.

The dome assumed its final form once the return had been made from the 1912 drawings to the Renaissance-type dome suggested in 1911 and redefined in 1920 and 1923. The partners were fully aware of the extent to which the design success of both the Legislative Building and the group plan was dependent on their ability to deal with the tremendous technical and compositional problems (and potential) of the dome. And though, even as late as 1925, they continued to ponder its implications, there were to be no significant changes at completion from what had been decided in 1923.

It was a splendid success. The drum, round and quite plain except for some horizontal reveals, was the base for a colonnade of thirty-two free-standing and pilastered columns, the pilasters being paired columns and piers as part of the buttress system of the dome with two free-standing columns between each bay. Here the architects repeated the Corinthian order, though with a different interpretation than on the porticoes—heavier, thicker in details, with pronounced volutes. There seems to be a more than coincidental similarity between these capitals and those at the familiar Roman Temple of Vesta in Tivoli. Did the partners remember seeing them in their travels or in a contemporary source book? Given the height of the location, the detail reads well from a distance, a good choice. The entablature that the columns support maintains that same spirit with the shades and shadows, lights and darks of its overhang, dentil moulding, consoles, and cheneaux. Above are panels of swags between shallow consoles above the buttresses, and beyond is the dome itself, ribbed to suggest structural utility with a pattern of reveals but otherwise plain. This wreath of detail from which springs the formal simplicity of the dome is impressive testimony to the architects' skill in manipulating their ornament budget for maximum visual return. The lantern completes the ensemble and is the nearest thing to whimsy that partners appear to have indulged in: a confection of balustrade, Corinthian columns, narrow arches, advancing and receding entablatures, consoles, frieze, and curved conical roof topped with a large stone ball. Its enthusiasm was a fitting climax to the crescendo of building and dome, their architectural fillip. Yet for all its playfulness, Sir Christopher Wren, a possible inspiration for the lantern, managed similar devices for his steeples with even more exuberance.

The dome's lantern

Two lanterns designed by Sir Christopher Wren: St. Michael Royal (1714) with St. Paul's (1659–1710) in the background

The structures at the corners of the dome platform had a much more uncertain history, which is curious since their role was clearly so subordinate and accessory to the dome, whose design had progressed with relative serenity. The evidence of the 1911 drawings is too obscure to determine Wilder and White's intentions at that date; the 1912 revisions, however, show no such features at all since the dome was shown rising abruptly out of the uniform roofline of the building. But the return in 1920 to a Renaissance-type dome saw the introduction of open Doric-columned corner tourelles with square plans and topped with stepped pyramids supporting shallow bronze urns. They had been chosen to ease the visual transition from the dome to its square base, but they also contributed to the design's general imbalance between its parts.

Nineteen twenty-three saw Wilder and White still studying the dome and its partnership with building and group, and explaining their preoccupation to the committee:

As we have stated in our previous reports, the problem lies in the relationship of a comparatively small building to a dome proportioned to the entire group. . . . [By] means of the square masonry base rising about the building, the dome is sufficiently separated from the lower work, to permit the latter being treated in scale with the other buildings in the group.[6]

No mention is made of tourelles, but we do know from examining various stages of design development that the partners continued to puzzle over them. The 1923 drawings (see pages 56 and 57) had round-domed tourelles on square plans, following the precedent of the Rhode Island Capitol. It was this 1923 design that was featured in the plaster model that the committee asked the architects to build and ship to Olympia for local appreciation of the project. Other experiments were tried; construction drawings of May 1925 moved away from the open tourelle and toward solid-faced masonry pyramids or pylons topped with bronze triumphal urns. Perhaps Wilder and White were aware of the capitols of Mississippi (1901–1903) and Kentucky (1910), two contemporaries with similar problems that used variations of elevated urns. But these too were rejected, for in April 1926 the partners wrote Johnston telling him "The corner pavilions however, will have to wait until we can give them the necessary study without holding up more pressing work."[7]

The procrastination began to be the source of some project gossip. T. L. Grant, an inspector nominally reporting to the committee but in practice acting in Governor Hartley's wary interests, sent one of his chatty communiques to the Governor in June mentioning that

I forgot to tell you about the Pylons for which the contractors have no details and cannot complete the outside of the building until next winter if there is much more delay on same. Details were promised months ago and they are very anxious to finish [in] this kind of weather. According to the contract the stone work was to be delivered 6/15/26. Can't expect contractors to keep up their job unless the state maintains its contract with the stone contractors.[8]

Almost simultaneously the architects were explaining to the committee the background and reasons for their delay:

. . . we are not wholly satisfied with the effect of either of the designs which we have tried out [for the pylons], and we would much prefer to give the matter further study before reaching a decision. We know of no dome in which features of this kind have been wholly satisfactory and they are such an important factor in the general effect, that we want them to be nearly right as possible.

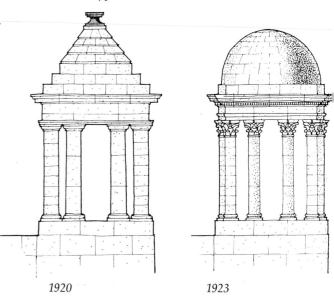

Design development phases for the dome's corner tourelle/pylon treatment

1920   1923

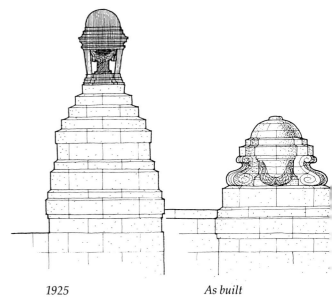

1925   As built

Plaster model of the Legislative Building, ca. 1925

On account of the curvature of the dome itself, their relationship to it and to the building is constantly changing, depending upon the point of view and what appears satisfactory in one position is not equally so in another. Of the two models now at Olympia the first in the form of open pavilions adds to the importance of the building, but to that extent tends to dwarf the dome; while the second design of more solid type adds to the scale of the dome but does not tie in so well with the building, and we hope to find a compromise between the two.

The delay in the decision regarding these features does not hold up any other work necessary to the proper occupation of the building by the next Legislature, the only risk being delay to a point where the hoist and scaffolding at the south entrance cannot be removed, and we hope to arrive at a satisfactory solution in ample time to erect these and remove the scaffolding by the end of the year. We feel that the importance of their correct design would warrant even the possible slight inconvenience and unsightly appearance of this scaffolding during the next session, for after all the building is being erected for the future, but we would naturally be subject to the instructions of the Committee in this respect. . . .

We trust that the Committee will realize that the further study we wish to give is entirely at our own expense and only with a view to satisfy ourselves that we have done the best possible. We trust you will also appreciate that in matters of design time is a very uncertain factor and a solution may come in a day or not for weeks. The nature of the work as pointed out in our letter of May 25th, has required a very unusual degree of personal attention, and we are doing our utmost to meet the situation in the most satisfactory way.[9]

Grant was still reporting to the governor at the end of August that work on the lantern was nearing completion, "which will finish every thing outside except the four Pylons for which the stone cutters have no details as yet. Hope they will be forthcoming soon?"[10] Again he had anticipated the architects, for in their letter of September 2 to the committee they announced:

We are glad to report that we have arrived at a satisfactory design for the corner pylons at the dome, which combines the advantages of each of the previous designs without their drawbacks. The work is now under way and we wish to express our appreciation of your allowing us the necessary time for study.

What they had decided was to retain the idea of the solid corner pylons but to give them a heavier mass and lower profile than those of 1925. Each pylon was given its own base on which were four strongly defined volutes paired at cross angles to each other and supporting a semicircular domed form. No classical or modern American models come to mind. It appears the architects were cut loose from Roman or Renaissance precedent, found no solutions at home that satisfied them, and so arrived independently at one of their own. It works well; the mass and scale are sufficient to ease the transition from the platform to the dome and to establish the pylons' own place in the scheme without intruding upon the primacy of the dome.

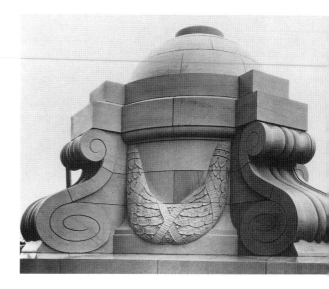

Corner pylon as built

The building's interiors are consistent with the architects' exterior decisions. There is the same correctness and economy of detail, restraint in what is offered but elegance in what is there, a degree of understatement unusual for a type of building too often given to overkill. But the building lacks warmth, both internally and externally. There is an austerity that comes in part from a certain academic rigidity in its design, in part from the economics that controlled it. The architects had hoped the state would be more generous in its commitment to collaboration with the other arts. Provisions were made for heroic sculptures on either side of the north stairways leading up to the Corinthian-columned main entrance, which would have above it the richness of a sculptured pediment. But except for the column capitals, none of this was to be. What did get included—the cheneaux of the cornice, the carvings of entablature, and the friezes on the platform of the dome and the dome itself—are reminders of the humanizing detail that is missing elsewhere.

There are similar problems inside. The marble and unpainted plaster of the principal public spaces—the rotunda, the State Reception Room, the two legislative chambers, and the main circulation areas in particular—are monochromatically bare and dull. The viewer misses what was planned but never delivered: the play of color and gilding that would have brought vibrance and contrast to the walls and three-dimensional patterning of coffered ceilings, friezes, cornices, and mouldings, all correctly formed and richly stated but unenhanced by those potentials. Missing too are the murals which, in balanced partnership with the architecture, would have lent their pictorial presence, color, pattern, warmth, and interest to great wall areas that instead are voids awaiting completion. After all, the American Renaissance (with Olympia's Legislative Building as a late bloomer of the genre) was intended as a union of all the arts—architecture, painting, sculpture, glass, fabrics—in celebration of the vitality of the designed environment. If Wilder and White's building seems to us too austere and aloof, most of the fault lies with the clients who withheld these collaborative means for its being more humane.

These observations are merely caveats, shortcomings in supportive areas rather than crucial ones, easily corrected had the client's will been there—or were we in our day to fill the vacuum and complete the task.* These frailties, beyond the responsibility and intent of the architects, cannot be allowed to detract from the recognition the partners clearly earned for the excellence of their achievement in Olympia.

Happily, these deficiencies are now being corrected. After almost sixty years, interior painting and lighting of the dome and rotunda were realized in 1986. This is a first step towards the finishing of other major public spaces: legislative chambers, state reception room, vestibules, and corridors. This awakening through the magic of color will bring renewed appreciation to this somewhat subdued state treasure.

Nevertheless, metaphorically that achievement is uncomfortably reminiscent of the dying apple tree that puts out a splendid crop in its last season, never to bear fruit again. For by 1928 the American Renaissance was poignantly close to its end as a creative era. Forces were already well advanced in Europe, poised to pick up momentum in our own country, which would discredit the design foundations on which Wilder and White's group plan had been based. Already presaged by the work of Gropius and van der Rohe abroad and by Louis Sullivan and Frank Lloyd Wright here at home, architecture's Modern Movement was soon to be influentially heralded by New York's new Museum of Modern Art at its opening exhibition in 1929, followed by another exhibition in 1932.

Nebraska's state capitol provides a revealing parallel. In Lincoln and Olympia, during the same years, the same programmatic requirements were met with startlingly contrasting solutions. Both designs approached the problem in the familiar format of classicism: axial, balanced, and symmetrical. But Bertram G. Goodhue, in his interpretation of that language for Nebraska, chose an individualized vocabulary of form and detail that broke with the academic classicism to which Wilder and White remained loyal. Goodhue was no Sullivan or Wright, yet there was a ferment in his work which, had it continued (he died unexpectedly in 1924 at the age of 55), might have given him a reputation for architectural innovation. No similar potential was demonstrated in the careers of Wilder and White. Despite the artistic and technical achievement that the Olympia capitol group represents for them, their design competence would soon be in eclipse. And by the time it might have been possible for them to join in an emerging new architectural tempo, circumstances denied them an opportunity for that creative evolution.

Nebraska State Capitol, Lincoln (1920–1932). View of the north facade in 1947.

VIII. The Hartley Imbroglio

From our contemporary vantage point, so often shaken and thwarted as we are by legal challenges, work stoppages, indifferent performance, cost overruns, and production delays, construction of the Legislative Building appears to have progressed remarkably smoothly. Professional, technical, administrative, and personal associations that spanned the building's construction years were mostly correct, productive, and civilized. Construction moved from phase to phase on schedule and within budgets. Though expenses were substantial, they were met at no cost to the taxpayers of the state. While the legislature extended no carte blanche to the State Capitol Committee, its authorizations were reasonable, providing the project with sufficient funding to support most of its essentials as visualized by the architects and the committee. And in contrast to similar efforts in some other states, the history of the Legislative Building project was entirely free of scandal and relatively free even from hints of it.

But all was not as serene as it appeared. There were abrasive episodes, personal confrontations, displays of pique, and exchanges of accusations, all demonstrating that a public project involving large amounts of money, high visibility, great expectations, and political potential is a likely stage for playing out personal ambitions.

In the early years of the Legislative Building project, such potential was apparently unrealized. The State Capitol Committee's three members, Governor Louis F. Hart, State Auditor C. W. Clausen, and State Land Commissioner Clark V. Savidge, worked harmoniously together, operating almost as free agents in exercising their authority to carry out the legislature's mandate to complete the building. But this era of good feeling closed abruptly in 1925 with a change in the governorship and thus the chairmanship of the committee. The instrumentalist for the project's remaining years of cacophony was Governor Roland Hill Hartley.

The new governor was short in both stature (5′6″) and temper, feisty, profane, intelligent but ill educated, and an ambitious political animal. A narrowly Republican partisan, his reputation and 1924 campaign (his third for the office after two defeats) were founded on economy and business methods in government, the open shop, "Americanism," the evils of excess taxation, and an enthusiastic endorsement of the coincident campaign of Calvin Coolidge for the presidency. In the Washington of 1924, this had all the trappings of success, and he won the governorship handily.

Hartley had made a relatively late arrival in the state. Born in Canada in 1864, he lived as a young man in Minnesota. There his marriage to the daughter of his employer (the future governor of Minnesota) provided him with influential family ties and an excellent apprenticeship in a variety of business and managerial situations and in the operations and opportunities of the political system. In his own subsequent business and political careers, his citation of self-reliance and individualism as the fountainheads of his achievements conveniently overlooked the momentum he had gained from family paternalism.

It was due to association with his father-in-law's timber interests that in 1902, in his late thirties, he moved to the mill town of Everett. By 1910 he was the city's mayor, by 1914 a state legislator, and in 1916 he was waging his first campaign for the governorship as "an articulate and even flamboyant spokesman for the cast-iron Republican industrial conservatism he chose to defend. He never hesitated to give his opinions or attitudes about business, labor unions, social workers, reformers, society, the state or the nation."[1]

Since Hartley arrived in Olympia when state politics and the legislature were dominated by loyalties similar to his own, it is curious how quickly he became embroiled in conflict at all levels of government. His governorship was a unique record of quarrelsomeness which would contribute significantly to frustrating the ambitions of his program. His associations with the State Capitol Committee were symptomatic of the general acrimony that marked his eight years in the capital.

The three-man capitol committee had been exercising (and enjoying) its authority over the Legislative Building project since 1921, and both the state auditor, C. W. Clausen, and the land commissioner, Clark V. Savidge, elected officials in their own right as well as being the committee's other two members, had served as well on the old seven-member Capitol Commission. Not only, therefore, were the two likely to be defensive of their roles in the history of the project to date, but, though the governor was the committee's chairman, their two votes constituted a majority and could control committee processes. Thus, both human and constitutional circumstances made it unlikely that the new chairman would fit smoothly into committee procedures, even had he been a personality of Solomonic character—which Hartley was not.

In addition to his fellow committee members, there were other members of the state's official family who could—and would—be potential antagonists: Secretary of State J. Grant Hinkle, State Treasurer William Potts, and Attorney General John H. Dunbar. They, too, were elected officials, had their own politically independent constituencies, and were experienced practitioners in shaping state policy and administering state affairs.

Hartley was immediately suspicious. As he saw it, these officials with their years of experience in office had built empires that were independent of his authority; therefore they were likely to resist the reforms he hoped to institute in state government, and if threatened they could be expected to reinforce their positions through mutual support. Hartley's style isolated him from his colleagues, and his practices reinforced this cleavage.[2]

A similar atmosphere was created in his association with those much more immediately involved in the project: the architects, their representatives, and the various operators in the field. While his contact with these people was in most cases indirect, the abrasiveness of deliberations within the inner circle affected those beyond its closed doors.

Hartley viewed Wilder and White as presumptuous eastern architects who were outrageously overpaid for work which could more suitably have been done by locals. The complexity of the job itself and the four-day train trip that separated the architects' New York office and the Olympia site would in any event have contributed to administrative uncertainty. In spite of assistance from the associated architects of Bebb and Gould in Seattle and the presence of Johnston as the architects' on-site representative, hesitancies, delays, and misunderstandings were inevitable and were all exacerbated by the governor. At one point he noted suspiciously the "constant telegraphing back and forth between Wilder and Johnston about which I know nothing; there is constant intrigue and scheming all the time. I've got enough stuff on that fellow Wilder to put him where he belongs."[3] The intricacies and problems of such a large-scale project got little sympathy from Hartley, whose antennae twitched nervously in search of deficiencies, real or imagined, and who called to task those he considered responsible, making enemies as he went. As the vice president of the construction company holding the contract to the Legislative Building was to remark in a note to Johnston: "It sure makes a fellow believe there is no justice in this world when a guy like Wilder gets the bad breaks while a certain part of a horse who infests an office across the street walks about in a disgustingly hearty state of health."[4]

Yet, in his initial dealings with the committee, there was little expression by Hartley of any basic dissatisfaction with what had gone before and considerable evidence of his pride as the building moved into its final construction years. His role as it developed would instead be one of waspishness: making unsubstantiated charges of construction deficiencies, improper methods in selecting suppliers, and general extravagance—usually matters more of detail than of substance, some more substantial than others.

If the governor felt he was surrounded by hostile forces, then it was clear he would need to create positions supportive of his interests. Thus, both committee minutes and the press were soon noting his concern over inadequate project supervision. A Seattle newspaper reported:

Governor Hartley is asking for more supervision and inspection of the construction work on the new Capitol building. . . . Governor Hartley cited faults in the insurance building. . . . Because of this trouble in the insurance building, Governor Hartley indicated that extra supervision and care should be given the new capitol. The supervision and inspection now is up to the architects Wilder & White of New York who are represented by their associates, Bebb & Gould of Seattle. The architects have Jay Johnston as resident in charge.

It is understood that Governor Hartley did not question the efficiency of Johnston, but did make his suggestion [because the present contract had become] too big for any one man.[5]

The committee at its September 24, 1925, meeting moved for the hiring of "an assistant to Mr. Johnston to assist him on the work, seconded by Mr. Clausen and carried." Wilder subsequently wrote to the committee reminding it that "such inspector will be cautioned against giving any instruction to the contractor or to the individual workmen."[6] These powers were by contract reserved to the architects or their representatives.

The appointment of the governor's candidate, T. L. Grant of Everett, for the job proved to be of little benefit in easing Johnston's supervisory tasks. Though Grant was informed by the committee that he was to report to Johnston, in practice he was to be the governor's eyes and ears on the job. Thus, a note from Hartley to Grant:

From a conversation I had with one of the men working on the new Administration Building [sic], am worried as to the progress of the work there. Are the detailed plans coming along as they should. . . ? Please look into the affair and report to me at the earliest possible moment.[7]

And some typical communications from Grant to Hartley:

I heard from a friend that Carlyon [an important Olympia senator] asked if I was interfering in any way as state inspector. May have told you this before. Again I heard did this and that come from the state inspector, coming from Mr. Bebb, so there seems to be some kind of an understanding between them as they seem to be playing on the same string. . . .

I heard Mr. Johnston in speaking about a letter from the architects, saying they could delay the rotunda details, that that was not at the suggestion of the architect. Don't know who he meant but you might. . . .

I think Tifeny [sic] would be a good bet on the lighting fixtures, if they would bid it. I understand they were low on some other work that they bid, but the architects played Jackson for a favorite and brought it about so Jackson got the job.[8]

It seems to me that the letting of work around here according to the New York idea is absurd; a good sample of which would be to have let the legislative building on said plan, vis., two rooms so large for House and Senate, building so big on ground; dome so high, including lantern. *All bid the same price.* Then, I (architect) and the Capitol Committee will decide which plan we like the best and award contract, I the architect, to take the six per cent commission—simple, isn't it? Same with light fixtures, furniture, etc., etc. I take the per cent; you do the work.[9]

I notice that all outlets for drains around building are choked up with fir needles, both on the terrace around the building and on roof of same, and the only way I know of to avoid same is to cut down the trees that surround grounds, all of which will blow down sooner or later.*[10]

Fortunately, many of these trees were allowed to remain, and still form a splendid setting southwest of the Legislative Building and around the Governor's Mansion.

Hartley's first chance to exploit the services of his informant with sufficient substance to appear in the records is found in a notation in the committee's minutes of July 8, 1926:

The Governor called attention to a report by Mr. T. L. Grant, the Committee's Inspector, to the effect that serious defects were showing up in the stone work on the Legislative Building. . . .

The assistant Secretary was instructed to write by night letter, Wilder & White informing them of the defects and asking Mr. Wilder to come to Olympia at once.

This was a typical ploy, demanding Wilder's immediate return to answer Hartley's charges. The incident played out through the following sequence, and was not unlike other storms blown up periodically by the chairman:

July 8: Johnston wired Wilder that Bebb suggests "stalling your leaving" with the likelihood "that explanation can be given tomorrow so that committee will rescind wire calling you at this time."

July 9: By return wire Johnston was informed that Wilder had "wired Mister Savidge fully regarding settlement."

July 13: The committee minutes noted that "it was decided that Mr. Wilder could use his own judgment as to whether he should come to Olympia at once, as requested by the Committee, or wait until the 1st of August as originally intended."

August 14: Wilder made his regularly scheduled return to Olympia in August. On August 14 he reported in a letter to White:

You will note that the interior cracks follow very closely those on the exterior and the only open cracks are certain of those which run vertically and in no case are over 3/64 of an inch. All vertical cracks not noted are hair cracks in most cases difficult to follow except on close examination in a strong light. The horizontal cracks on the inside are no wider than those on the outside showing practically no tilt in the wall and in no case do the cracks run lower than the line of the adjoining flat roofs. . . .

You will note by our report to the Committee that we can only account for these cracks by expansion of the stone cornice which is most exposed to the sun and there are not even hair cracks visible above the line of the brackets.

August 24: Gunvald Aus Co., the firm's New York engineering consultant, confirmed that the cracks were not caused by foundation settlement but were the result of unequal expansion; the company did "not believe that there is any thing to be done as nothing more can happen."[11]

And so the cracks incident passed with no known further recorded references to it.

The crisis of the furniture was more convoluted, played to a much larger audience, and spanned years rather than weeks. The first hints that the governor had a low tolerance for the subject of furnishings came in early 1926 when initial efforts were being made to establish furniture needs for the new building. No difficulties were encountered until the consultant, a Mr. Grainger, reached the governor, who was asked

what he might think necessary for his private office in the new building. At about this place in their conversation the Governor wanted to know what Grainger had to do with the furniture and if he (the Governor) had to go over and measure up the rooms in order to see what he needed, then he could see *no reason for paying a commission to an architect.*[12] [emphasis added]

As chairman of the committee, he had had earlier contact with the matter, the committee already having in hand the $600,000 that the legislature had authorized for the purchase of furnishings. As previously described, the architects and the committee had decided that at least for key public rooms and spaces standard items would not do. For those locations manufacturers were asked to bid on special design and quality standards. Hartley had been a party to these arrangements.

The other members of the committee were therefore considerably bewildered when at their meeting of September 30, 1926, intended to include the signing of the furniture contracts, Hartley blasted the gathering with accusation of "extravagance and waste."

The further we proceed with the method adopted for securing bids for furnishing the equipment of the new capitol building, the more certain it appears to me that our procedure is wrong and can only work out to the detriment of the state.

Instead of calling for bids for the necessary furnishings on a competitive basis we are asking three concerns how much they will give us for $568,900 upon plans and specifications which apparently stifle rather than promote competition.[13]

Wilder, who was in attendance, attempted to reassure the chairman that the method being used for furniture bidding was the same as for the building itself: manufacturers would have to satisfy design and quality standards in their proposals and be judged accordingly. To rely on conventional furniture acquisition methods for a building of this stature would simply subject the procedure to indefinite quality standards and second rate bidders. As Wilder had explained in an earlier letter to the committee:

The proposal of the Weary and Alford Company is an excellent example of a practice unfortunately so frequent in public bidding that it is extremely difficult to persuade reputable firms to figure.

The notice to bidders and the specifications are always very definite that no proposal varying in form or substance from that called for will be considered, but some firm will usually come in at the last minute with a proposal on a different basis and by means of a combination of specific samples attractively displayed and clever salesmanship will either sweep the Committee off their feet or so confuse the issue as to prevent a decision on the other proposals. . . .

We find as we expected that [Weary and Alford] have disregarded not only the provision for separate consideration of divisions but of the allowances themselves, so far as can be determined by adding the totals arrived at in multiplying their unit prices by the number of each item. . . . We presume the above will be sufficient to show the futility of attempting to consider this a bid competition in any way with the other proposals.[14]

Weary and Alford's Olympia representative was J. A. Clorety, a personal friend of Hartley. By now the committee and the issue were both sufficiently confused that no contract signing took place.

Hartley apparently came to feel he had an important political issue in hand, for he went public with it. Although he had just succeeded in arranging for the dismissal of the University of Washington's president, he chose to ignore that accomplishment in a fifteen-minute radio address to concentrate instead on the profligacy of the committee in its methods for acquiring the Legislative Building's new furniture:

A costumer, Governor Hartley said, is "a piece of lumber six feet long with four metal hooks on top," but they were priced at $157 each or "more than the price of two cows."

Some bidders offered waste baskets at $96 each and cuspidors at $447.75 each, while other bidders offered cuspidors at $3.50 each and waste-baskets at $10 a piece, the governor said. . . .

"As governor of this state and as chairman of the capitol committee, I do not propose to sanction such wasteful extravagance," he said.[15]

In spite of rebuttals, the governor found he had hit a responsive chord in the public. Both he and the press played upon it.

The charges of profligate extravagance which have been hurled by the governor, coupled with the accusation that unsound business methods were used in making purchases, have captured popular fancy to an even greater extent than the so-called timber, education and highway "rows,". . . In the hinterland, it is said, the Capitol is construed by Hartley followers as a "Temple to Mammon" rather than a "Monument to Representative Government." And even in the furthest places of the Commonwealth, "asked and bid" quotations on cuspidors, costumers and waste paper baskets are declared to constitute a principal topic of conversation.[16]

The *Everett News,* a Hartley champion, reported heatedly that

One of the largest and best known furniture houses in the country, a concern which has furnished many public buildings offered to furnish the new state capitol building down at Olympia. This firm brought in many samples, placed them in rooms to show what they were, and then placed its bid.

What happened? Architect Walter Wilder, for the state capitol committee, advised that the bid be rejected, and this was done, State Auditor Clausen and Land Commissioner Savidge, over the protest of Governor Hartley, went ahead with the awarding of the contracts and paid no more attention to this bid.

The company was Weary and Alford.

Why was the bid thrown out?

Because it was too low. This admission is made in the letter of Architect Wilder to the capitol committee. . . .

[Another bidder] showed this specification to some of the biggest monumental furniture men in the east. They were amazed that Washington would stand for it. It made them so suspicious, many of them, that they refused to compete. . . .

"The new capitol building will be literally stuffed with furniture," he says. . . . The state reception room of the capitol is supposed to be the most beautiful and dignified of them all. It is to be elegant. But the whole effect is going to be spoiled by too much furniture. Tables, desks, chairs, davenports, umbrella stands, and hat-racks will be jammed into it.

"There will be a chair in front of each column and a ridiculous splatter of gaudy furniture throughout the room.

"Then—travesty of travesties—there will be eight big brass spittoons to ruin whatever good effect might still remain!

"The man who figures out the furniture needs must have believed everybody out here chewed tobacco and that it rained every day. Thousands could be accommodated with cuspidors at one time in the new capitol if all the cuspidors are finally bought. And there'll be umbrella stands enough for regiments of wet politicians. . . .

"No matter what you may think of Hartley on other matters, we men in the furniture trade know he is one hundred percent right in this matter when he charges incompetence, extravagance, and unbusinesslike methods."[17]

But the *Aberdeen Daily World* took a more benign stance on the issue.

It may be assumed without argument that Mr. Savidge and Mr. Clausen have the interests of the people of the state at heart as much as the governor. . . and that in awarding contracts for the furnishings for the new capitol they were acting in accordance with their best judgment and the advice of experts and in keeping with the furnishings the splendid new capitol should have.

The people do not expect this building to be furnished with wooden benches, flimsy desks, calico curtains, rag rugs, and cane bottom chairs. They do expect it to be furnished appropriately in the character of the building and the function it is to serve. They have taken pride in the state buildings already erected and they will take pride in the new capitol, for which they have waited for many years. . . . The fact is that the new capitol building has been built at a minimum of cost, much less than any comparable structure in the country, and that it is a credit to the designers and to the people.[18]

To prevent the signing of the contracts, the chairman refused to call a meeting of the committee. Finally, in exasperation, Savidge and Clausen in December held a meeting and signed the contracts without him.* Though the contracts were further delayed by a court challenge related to the use of timber income for furnishings, the Supreme Court held in favor of such usage, and furniture manufacture and delivery finally began moving forward.

But the furniture's arrival only raised the confrontation to a higher level of sound and fury, ranging from familiar themes of selection procedures and extravagant costs to design and workmanship. Hartley, not wanting to be "a party to wild and profligate expenditures in furnishing the new Capitol Building,"[19] refused to sign any payment vouchers unless compelled to do so by the courts. (His critics thought his fastidiousness had more to do with preparing for his 1928 re-election campaign.)

The chairman stated that the furniture installed in his department in the Legislative Building was unsatisfactory owing to the fact that the chairs were too high and the tables and desks had square corners instead of being round as he supposed had been ordered. Attention was called to the fact that the Committee had approved this furniture on February 16 and that Wilder and White had furnished descriptions both written and photographic of the furniture that was to be installed, and as these had been approved by the Committee it would be impossible to change them at this late date.[20]

Johnston had written to Wilder and White on June 21 describing a similar scene that also gave some indication of the acidity of personal relationships in the committee.

Saturday† about noon the committee came over to the new building to inspect the sample of filing cabinets and the governor asked that they come into his office and see the furniture, which they did. . . all he did was to kick on everything in general; they weren't comfortable, and they were so big no one could sit in them, and their feet touch the floor. . . . I tried to tell him all changes had been approved by the committee, but you might as well stand back and say nothing. The only good part was that Hinkle [the Secretary of State] said to him: 'Well, governor, we wont always have such a small man for governor,' which can be taken in more ways than one.

*The meeting was held in a committee room off the governor's office; the governor remained in his own office during the session.

†On the same date, June 21, the state supreme court handed down its decision, authorizing Clausen to sign furniture vouchers for the committee, instead of the governor.

Governor Roland H. Hartley and some of the offending items of the Legislative Building's furnishing contract. Photograph by Vibert Jeffers, © 1985 by Susan Parish/First Light Media Collection, Olympia.

The governor, however, continued to grumble about the quality and especially the expense of the furniture and in August, his campaign for re-election now steaming up, he took his case, and the furniture, to the people:

Onto a truck he loaded various pieces of furniture taken from the new capitol building and, with a large number of "Hartley candidates," stumped the state demonstrating to the voters in sideshow fashion the extravagance and waste being purveyed upon the people by his opponents. The star attraction of the Hartley museum of capitol curiosities was a sixty-seven pound hammered brass cuspidor, one of four designed for the corners of the capitol rotunda. To this item the governor ascribed a price of $100. Several other articles, such as an ornamental chair from the Senate chamber and a hat rack of disputed price, were also presented to the public view. The procession was rapidly named the "Hartley cuspidor caravan."[21]

The "Hartley candidates" were all selected by him to run against the officials who in the past four years had opposed him, especially Savidge and Clausen. In a style remarkably presaging the techniques used nationwide in the early 1950s, he would feature a mysterious black bag, which, he informed his audiences, contained evidence to put the "rotton bunch," especially Savidge and Clausen, in the penitentiary; but he never revealed just what that dark information added up to nor did he press charges to bring the "criminals" to justice.[22]

Though his own re-election efforts were successful, none of the Hartley candidates succeeded in ousting any of the "rotton bunch," all of whom returned to join him for another four years in the administration of state affairs, including completion of the Legislative Building.

In the meantime, a further complication developed that involved all parties in new acrimony. The building had been administratively turned over to the state in mid-1927 and had come under the direction of Olaf L. Olsen, director of the Department of Business Control and a Hartley appointee. Johnston, writing for the architects, in September brought to the committee's attention that there was "no systematic procedure for Heating and Ventilating the Building. . . . We are bringing the above to your attention for fear that the furniture will be greatly damaged unless some immediate action is taken to remedy the condition of dampness throughout the building."[23]

The committee quickly alerted Olsen to this potential, citing Johnston's letter and noting the dangers to the building, which was not yet completely dried out, and to its furnishings. In August the committee had approved a motion for occupancy by state offices, but Hartley was insisting that the building could not be occupied until a full inventory of furnishings had been completed. The committee's letter continued:

You are, therefore, requested to allow the building to be immediately occupied by the state officers for whom it was intended and also to take immediate steps to see that [it] is properly heated and ventilated in order that this damage above referred to both to the building and to the furniture may not continue.

Mr. Savidge moved that the letter be adopted and transmitted to Mr. Olsen. . . .

The Chairman protested in connection with the above letter to Mr. Olsen as follows:

I absolutely protest the document as false, misleading, and impossible of carrying out, for the reason that the furniture is not yet listed; the inventory is not made, which is necessary before the occupancy of the building. I protest this untrue, misleading and a star-chamber document made before the inspection of the building this morning.

The motion carried with the Chairman voting "No" and stating that the building would not be occupied until the inventory now being taken by the Department of Business Control was fully completed.[24]

Olsen replied the next day that heat was in fact being maintained "at about 70 degrees" and that it was the general condition of the building, not any failure of his part to provide heating and ventilating, that could affect the furniture.

Johnston did not agree. On October 11 he wired Wilder and White of his concerns, informing them of where the specific defects were showing up and their nature—how desks, chairs, and tables in the Senate and House chambers and in the "ladies [state] reception room" had joints opening up, raised graining, and sprung panels. He asked that a representative of the manufacturers be sent to investigate as soon as possible to determine the causes.

Wilder replied that the architects were unable to account for such a development, *"and particularly as to why it should come up just before election"* [emphasis added].

I wish you would write me confidentially if you have heard any rumor of any condition at the building that might account for it, although they would have to be so serious that it hardly seems possible. If it will make it easier for you, you can write such a letter longhand and we will return a copy of it for your records.[25]

Johnston replied that he too was at a loss but then went on to note rather obliquely the potential damage to furniture that he had already recognized in September. The defects were appearing almost exclusively

on the third and fourth floors which as you know are unoccupied. Whether the State has given these floors the proper attention as to heating and ventilating I am unable to say. Even though this space has not been given the proper attention it seems to me impossible that this furniture should show the numerous defects now apparent. . . .

On Monday evening October 9th at a Masonic meeting Mr. Collins the head Janitor informed me the desks in the House Chamber were showing defects and we decided to inspect them the next morning before I left for Seattle. At that time no one else was aware of the defects; however, Mr. Collins at some time during the day notified the Department of Business Control, and they in turn notified each member of the Capitol Committee of the existing conditions.[26]

CAPITOL BOARD'S ACTION CALLED DISGRACE
Executive Charges Clausen and Savidge with Holding Star Chamber Sessions on Landscaping
RIGHTS TRAMPLED ON[36]

Committee minutes for August 20, 1929, give further expression of Hartley's concerns:

Now you are trying to hide [the capitol group] behind a screen. That means just one more thing, a little more graft for the Olmsted Brothers so they can collect. [Dawson, the Olmsted man on the campus plan] gets four per cent on all extra cost [for revising the plans]. That is what he is after. The more he can make it cost the better it will please him and the people don't want it. Everybody I talk to, there isn't a soul but says "Give us a simple grade and a lawn down here that we can see these buildings." The people have a right to see them, but you are diminishing them, and hiding them and putting them over here apparently in a swamp back of a hill from the travelling public. I can't understand it.

The press and the public were mostly supportive of the governor. In general, both endorsed the idea of eliminating any topography and landscaping that would interrupt sweeping views toward the Capitol group and the Legislative Building's dome. Finally, the committee's approval for destroying the old Stevens residence* removed that building's awkward impact on the plan, and new grading was done. Dunham returned to Highway Department duty, and by 1930 vistas from both Eleventh Street and Capitol Way were opened up and the planting scheme that one finds on campus today was established. The people got their simple grade and a lawn.

*Approval was given—but not without a struggle, anticipating the preservation confrontations of a few decades later.

And so the committee quarreled and bickered through the last years of its responsibility for completing the Legislative Building. Even from sixty years' distance, it is possible to understand the majority's frustrations as it attempted to work its way through these and many other episodes that the chairman imagined, created, and exaggerated en route to a finished project.

It is also possible to recognize that the chairman was by nature remarkably ill-prepared for a role into which his political successes had moved him. And even had a governor more gifted in human relationships than Hartley been chairman, it would no doubt have been some time before the closely knit associations that had previously developed among the committee, other elected officials, and the architects and their associates would loosen sufficiently to make a place for the new boy on the block. But Hartley gave them no assistance in adjusting to his presence. His cocky personal style, his limited education and his disdain for it in principle, his pungent vocabulary and the unreliability of what he said, his self-imposed isolation from his peers even before it was clear that he was unwelcome, and the cronies he included among the appointments he controlled were all bound to repel those proper bureaucrats† with whom he had been cast to carry out the public's business. Thus, his every move caused them to close ranks more tightly— with the governor locked out instead of being invited in.

†An exception was John Dunbar, the attorney general, whose drunken driving arrests jeopardized his 1928 re-election campaign, though not enough to defeat him.

Night view of the Legislative Building shortly after completion. Photograph by Vibert Jeffers, © 1985 by Susan Parish/ First Light Media Collection, Olympia.

Thankfully, the building itself was somehow aloof from these human frailties, and at some unidentifiable moment it was suddenly seen to be splendidly complete.* Perhaps it was the night of January 17, 1929, when Hartley was being inaugurated for his second term, and the building's great dome, illuminated by searchlights, could be seen white against a dark sky or in rippled reflection across the night-black waters of Puget Sound.†

*No formal dedication ceremony ever took place. The legislature had appropriated $10,000 for the occasion, but the governor vetoed it. The Daily Olympian *recorded March 28, 1928, as the date the legislature officially occupied the building.*

†Fifty-six years later, on January 16, 1985, another governor, Booth Gardner, was inaugurated in that same setting, and for the first time in the Legislative Building's history it was also the setting of the traditional inaugural ball. The Seattle Times *reported the following day on the "4000 cheering revelers" whose presence was strange but, one likes to think, not unwelcome in the great rotunda, on the stairs, in the chambers and halls as the building adjusted to yet another generation of service to the state.*

IX. The Years That Followed

At last the State of Washington had its Legislative Building, a new home for the legislature which met there for its first full session in the winter of 1929. In the meantime, the architects had returned to their offices, Wilder to New York, Bebb to Seattle. Johnston was the last to leave the project, surrendering his master key to Olsen and then attending his last meeting of the committee on February 18, 1928. It was an unsigned letter of February 20, 1929, to Wilder, possibly from Bebb, which stated what might well have come from all of them:

I am through and damned glad of it. And I still can look back upon the eighteen years service I have given the State in so many directions unashamed and criticism and contumely considering the source only excite gleeful chuckles. And don't forget the fight of all the Kilkenny cats rolled into one is in my veins. May the gods preserve me from any other State work under the present administration.

Nineteen twenty-nine was an ominous year for everyone, but it was particularly foreboding for three of the principals* who had most directly participated in the project. For Wilder and White there was a special irony. This unknown firm had dared much and had brought to completion a project handsomely conceived in form and detail. Technically demanding as well as costly in the dollars of its day, it was singularly free of crisis and scandal—Governor Hartley's interference notwithstanding. Surely this was the launching of a brilliant national career. Yet for the firm it came to nothing. Wilder had returned sick to New York, and in 1930, when the partnership was dissolved, he retired to Suffern, New York. There, alone and in poor health, he committed suicide in 1934.

White, like most architects, struggled through the depression years. He found private work intermittently, and served as a consultant for the Vermont State government in the mid-1930s and in Washington, D.C., in the early days of federal housing. During World War II he was more active, in association with a large New York architecture and engineering firm that handled very large-scale public works both on the East Coast and in Hawaii. He continued to commute between New York and his Plainfield, New Jersey, home into his mid-eighties, when at last he retired. He died in 1966, at the age of eighty-nine. The untimely demise of the firm of Wilder and White is one of the unnoted repercussions of the Great Depression.

For Johnston, events similarly blighted the promising future for which he was now so broadly prepared. He was forty-three when he left the project to re-enter a construction market that had almost entirely closed down. Remaining in Olympia, he was to experience several years of under-employment, then a gradual pickup that sustained him until he, like White, was swept into the flood of wartime construction. His last working years were with the Port of Olympia, supervising its various construction projects. He was in retirement at the time of his death in 1969.

*The fourth, Governor Hartley, was defeated for re-election in the Roosevelt landslide of 1932; rejected again by the voters in 1936, he remained in reluctant retirement in Everett until his death in 1952.

We sometimes reflect on the tragedy of a life's promise cut short by an untimely death. The coincidence of the closing of the Legislative Building project and the beginning of the 1930s depression is a reminder that, even when life goes on, its promise can still be vulnerable. Each of these men suddenly had an opportunity of enormous potential, and many years remaining in his career to realize it. They succeeded splendidly, only to be blocked by circumstances in which their talents were no longer required, or at least not at the level at which they were prepared to offer them. By the time the nation and its architects were again joined as a creative force for designing and building, Wilder was gone and neither White nor Johnston was positioned to pick up where together they had left off.

It was not by coincidence that those two elders in the late 1950s and early 1960s were drawn together for visits to the maturing grounds of the Capitol campus and its buildings, especially the Legislative Building, where they wandered from floor to floor through its great and lesser spaces reminiscing about the people and events that brought it all about. Washington State's audacious state capitol was, after all—though prematurely—their finest hour, where "the American Renaissance in state capitol building reached its climax,"[1] here at the outer limits of the nation on the shores of lower Puget Sound.

The character established by the Wilder and White group plan and the completion of its centerpiece, the Legislative Building, meant that any subsequent campus work would—as intended—be accessory to it. Though that work has seen an extension of space and facilities far beyond any dimensions envisioned by the authors of the group plan, the success of the original idea has nevertheless remained vindicated and paramount. Further development was only slowed, not blocked, by the economic depression of the 1930s. Beginning again in 1934, it has continued intermittently ever since.

The first new construction was the Highways Building (now known as the Institutions Building). It established a double break with tradition, being built outside the group plan and in an architectural style different from the one Wilder and White had determined. Set apart, southwest of the Insurance Building, instead of sharing its predecessors' Wilkeson stone classical monumentality, it was built in a style best described as "brick anonymous 1930s modern." Its greatest fault is that it exists at all. Perhaps its relatively modest cost and years of write-off will facilitate a decision for its early removal.

Both 1937 and 1940 saw a return to the group plan and its architecture with the construction, respectively, of the Social Security Building (for many years called the Public Lands Building, and renamed the John E. Cherberg Building by action of the Capitol Committee in 1985) and the Transportation Building (today's House Office Building). Located at angles to each other and south of the Legislative Building, they conform fully to Wilder and White's group plan format.

Aerial view of the Capitol group and Olympia, ca. 1928

Aerial view of Capitol group in the 1940s

The late 1940s were to include beautification of the expanse at the base of the Capitol group site to its north and west. The partners' plan saw this area as a grand water feature, and if the tide was in this was more or less its image. But low tides exposed it as a great plane of mud flats down whose length meandered the somewhat leisurely channel of the Deschutes River. Authorized by legislative action, work proceeded toward the westward extension of Fifth Avenue to parallel existing Fourth Avenue and its bridge, both now connecting downtown Olympia to the "Westside" and beyond. The project also included construction of a dam, the ensemble thereby creating a permanent body of water, Capitol Lake. Substantially completed by 1951, this new visual and recreational amenity became an appropriate setting for the acropolis of the Capitol group which it now so handsomely supported.

An unfortunate presence outside the group plan but adjoining it was established with completion in 1956 of the General Administration Building, built on a site in a new expansion area northward across Eleventh Street (now Eleventh Avenue). It is difficult to identify any positive visual contribution that it makes to the campus environment.

By 1956 it was also clear that, contrary to earlier expectations, the campus would require additional acreage. The Capitol Committee, seeking professional guidance toward a more systematic approach to this expansion, turned to a Seattle firm, Puget Planners, which recommended that the campus grow south to Eighteenth Avenue between Capitol Way and the bluffs overlooking the Deschutes Basin. This plan would have provided almost twenty-five additional acres for future building.

There were reservations about any additional move to the south, however. The cost of acquiring houses of some substance (and perhaps the political clout of their residents) encouraged a search for alternatives. The Capitol Committee turned next to architect Paul Thiry of Seattle, who in 1958 presented a plan that for the first time recommended an expansion across Capitol Way, breaking through the barrier which that main highway (U.S. 99) had for so long created as the eastern boundary of the campus. Thiry recognized the strength of both the plan and the architecture of the existing campus, but realized that future expansion would require a break. An east campus development could respect the past but at the same time allow for changing needs and circumstances. It would also ease access to the new interstate freeway farther east.[2]

Thiry was also chosen as architect for the new State Library (1961) whose location would close the vista south from the Legislative Building, on land already within campus holdings. Although this building does not conform stylistically to its immediate campus neighbors, its siting, handsome form, use of Wilkeson stone, and fine detailing make it a successful adjunct to the original group.

Thiry's campus plan may have broken the Capitol Way barrier, but early decisions about what was now known as the East Campus were made without any conformity to his specific recommendations. In 1961 and 1962 new state buildings were completed there, first the Employment Securities Building and then the Highway Licenses Building. They were followed by the Archive Building in 1964. None of these buildings maintained the architectural themes of West Campus structures, nor did their positions suggest any coordination with the intervening grounds west of Capitol Way to acknowledge the Olmsted Plan.

Olympia and the Capitol group in the late 1940s before work had started on the development of Capitol Lake; the tide is in.

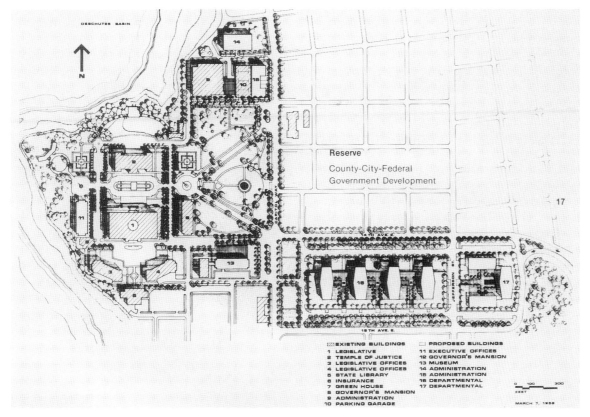

Paul Thiry plan for campus expansion, 1958

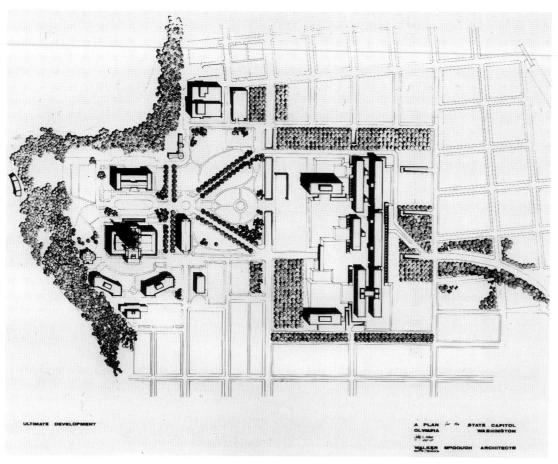

ULTIMATE DEVELOPMENT

A PLAN for the STATE CAPITOL
OLYMPIA   WASHINGTON

WALKER McGOUGH ARCHITECTS

Walker/McGough/Foltz development
plan for the Capitol campus, 1970

To overcome this *ad hoc* nature of the East Campus development, the committee in 1966 hired the Spokane firm of Walker/McGough/Foltz, Architects to create plans for future development. Their recommendations were to cover expansion of legislative and administrative functions, parking, and the location of a new Highways Building. On the basis of the firm's sequential studies, a comprehensive East Campus move was authorized by the legislature in 1967, and soon the large rectangular area of 48.5 acres bounded by Eleventh Avenue, Jefferson Street, and Maple Park was all state owned, creating a total campus area of 103 acres. Successive studies were summarized in a report entitled "Comprehensive Planning Study."[3]

The recommendations had little physical impact on the West Campus, nor was there much effort to achieve any degree of spatial and design unity with it. The main suggestion was that the Departments of Public Lands, Social Security, and Transportation be shifted to the East Campus, their two West Campus buildings to be converted to Senate and House offices. Today the former Transportation Building is the House Office Building, while Senate offices occupy the renamed Cherberg Building.

The East Campus plan proposed a complex of administrative buildings, plazas and lawns, a multi level underground parking garage, and extensive formal plantings to define campus boundaries. While certain visual alignments were noted between east and west, the two campuses were treated essentially as environmentally different generations with little in common except propinquity. The plan was the basis both for what developed on the East Campus in the busy construction years of the 1970s and for the design dichotomy that now appears to have been permanently built between them.

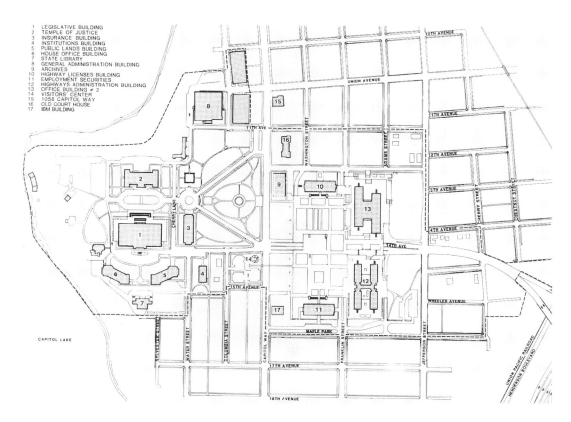

1 LEGISLATIVE BUILDING
2 TEMPLE OF JUSTICE
3 INSURANCE BUILDING
4 INSTITUTIONS BUILDING
5 PUBLIC LANDS BUILDING
6 HOUSE OFFICE BUILDING
7 STATE LIBRARY
8 GENERAL ADMINISTRATION BUILDING
9 ARCHIVES
10 HIGHWAY LICENSES BUILDING
11 EMPLOYMENT SECURITIES
12 HIGHWAYS ADMINISTRATION BUILDING
13 OFFICE BUILDING # 2
14 VISITORS' CENTER
15 1058 CAPITOL WAY
16 OLD COURT HOUSE
17 IBM BUILDING

*Existing buildings and
facilities, 1982*

*Aerial view of the Capitol
campus, 1976*

The Legislative Building was not immune from impacts during these later years, mostly due to two separate and severe earthquakes. The first was in 1949. Johnston returned to the site temporarily to assist in reconstruction work, including the dismantling of the dome's lantern to reinforce its structure and lighten its dead loads. The lantern's present glistening spire, a light metal replacement for the former weight of stone, is the unfortunate result of that effort. Then in 1965 came the second of the building's shakings. Although the consequences of that earthquake were less visible, they were far more complex and expensive, for the state determined that a thorough program of earthquake stabilization for the building was required.

Subsequently, all but eight of the dome's twenty-two tall windows, which on the exterior sat behind the dome's supporting colonnade, were filled in with concrete panels to give greater stability to the drum. Below, continuous transverse reinforced-concrete shear walls were carefully incorporated into the floor plans to add an important degree of lateral resistance to the structure without damaging the visual quality of major spaces. When this and other work was finally completed the state had spent $9,600,000 (some $2,808,000 more than the building's original cost).

Almost from the beginning both campuses have received a variety of improvements other than architectural and landscaping that have added to their interest in varying degrees. The first of these, the World War I memorial, was followed in 1940 by the placement across from the General Administration Building of an eighty-five-foot totem pole sculpted by Chief William Shelton and presented to the state by Snohomish County schoolchildren. In 1953 a fountain was built in the great lawned oval on the east-west axis of the West Campus. A copy of a fountain in the Tivoli Gardens of Copenhagen, it was another gift to the state.*

*Donated by the Olympia-Tumwater Foundation, Inc.

From these beginnings a significant collection of outdoor sculpture has evolved, in most cases the result of "percentage for art" legislation which requires that such investment of state funds be included in construction budgets. Today's campus thus displays the work of many prominent members of the art community.

The most recent architectural addition to the campus is the Visitors' Information Center, completed in 1981. A rather spontaneous gesture on the part of the 1979 legislature, its construction is a reminder of how vulnerable to piecemeal development the campus had become.

The election in 1980 of Governor John Spellman introduced an era of renewed interest in the campus in general and the Legislative Building in particular; happily, this enthusiasm was reaffirmed with the election of Governor Booth Gardner in 1980. The opportunity was recognized and grasped for deciding some fundamental questions affecting future state construction in Olympia and the role and character of the Capitol campus. Both the governor's office and the legislature joined in this initiative, the latter in its 1981 session authorizing the hiring of consultants to assist in the state's'search for such directions. Assisted by a Legislative Advisory Panel, a Capitol Campus Design Advisory Committee of design professionals, and key staff members of the Department of General Administration, the selected consultants, John Graham and Company of Seattle, prepared a comprehensive long-range plan for the future of the campus. Published in August 1982, "The Master Plan for the Capitol of the State of Washington" acknowledges the need of the campus "to be honored as an important environmental work of art."[4] The report's principles demonstrate how directions in the physical development of the campus can indeed enhance its future as such a monument.

Scaffolding for repair work on the dome following the 1949 earthquake

The Capitol group with the Tivoli Fountain in the foreground

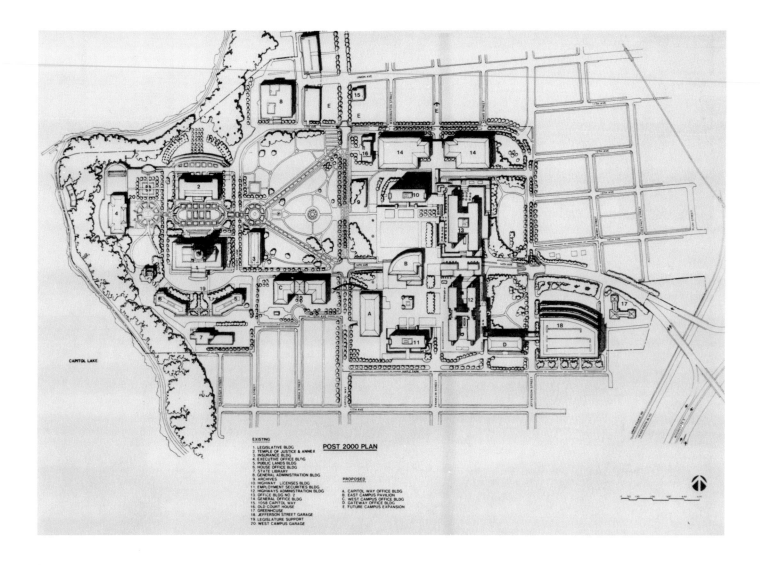

Post-2000 plan for the Capitol campus

But the master plan, properly, goes beyond the merely physical and establishes policy guidelines by which the campus can not only look splendid but function splendidly. An indication of the values observed in developing the plan is suggested by a paragraph in the report's Foreword:

From the first we have given special priority to the design and visual aspects of the campus. Its perceptual importance, not only as a grouping of buildings, but as a major design contribution to Olympia and as a symbol of government, has been paramount in our evaluating procedures. Thus, the treatment of existing buildings; location, height, and scale of any future buildings; the preservation, extension, and enhancement of existing spatial and landscape qualities and key vistas of the campus; and the design quality of the incremental but smaller elements of the campus environment such as art, lighting fixtures, and signage have all been included in our discussions and recommendations.

An affirmation of concern and commitment by the current administration under Governor Gardner is the decision of the legislature and the Department of General Administration to proceed with their painting and lighting plan and program for the Legislative Building's major interior spaces. First results can now be enjoyed in the building's rotunda and dome; the work was dedicated with full ceremony on January 15, 1987.

View of the rotunda and the dome,
displaying their 1986 interior finishing.
Photograph by Gant W. Eichrodt;
courtesy of the Washington State
Legislature Office of Facilities Planning.

    With these efforts, and the commitment of the people and government of
the state to honoring them, we can reaffirm the vision and achievement for
Washington's state capitol initiated in 1911 by the Wilder and White group
plan. There could be no better way to celebrate our coming hundredth
anniversary of statehood in 1989 than such a dedication.

Detail, bronze doors, north portico

Notes

Introduction

1. Henry-Russell Hitchcock and William Seale, *Temples of Democracy: The State Capitols of the USA*, p. 3.
2. Arthur S. Beardsley, "Early Attempts to Locate the Capital of Washington Territory," *Pacific Northwest Quarterly* 32, no. 3 (July 1941): 241.
3. Clark V. Savidge, "Brief Outline of the History of Washington's State Capitol Group," p. 15.
4. Clark V. Savidge, "Uncle Sam Gave Washington Her Capitol," *The Washingtonian, a State Magazine of Progress* 1, no. 3 (March 1928): 11, 42.

Chapter I. The Competition of 1893

1. State Capitol Commission [later State Capitol Committee, hereafter SCC], minutes for July 26, 1893.
2. SCC minutes for July 27, 1893.
3. Ibid.
4. SCC minutes for August 24, 1893.
5. J. A. Chewning, "William Robert Ware at MIT and Columbia," *Journal of Architectural Education* 33, no. 2 (November 1979): 26–27.
6. SCC, *First Biennial Report*, p. 12.
7. Ibid., p. 13.
8. Ibid., p. 14.
9. Ibid., p. 16.
10. Arthur S. Beardsley, "Later Attempts to Relocate the Capitol of Washington," *Pacific Northwest Quarterly* 32, no. 4 (October 1941): 432–33.
11. P. H. Carlyon, "From Shack to Palace," *The Washingtonian, a State Magazine of Progress* 1, no. 3 (March 1928): 44.

Chapter II. The Competition of 1911

1. Mardges Bacon, *Ernest Flagg*, pp. 112–19, 134–37.
2. SCC minutes for January 24, 1911.
3. SCC minutes for March 28, 1911.
4. *Seattle Times*, April 30, 1911.
5. American Institute of Architects, 1911, copy of resolution, Special Collections Division, Suzzallo Library, University of Washington, Seattle.
6. *Seattle Times*, April 30, 1911.
7. Ibid.
8. SCC minutes for April 29, 1911.
9. Ibid.
10. SCC minutes for July 31, 1911.
11. Copy of typewritten statement with Charles H. Bebb's initials, June 30, 1917, Special Collections Division, Suzzallo Library, University of Washington, Seattle.

Chapter III. The Wilder and White Entry

1. Various interviews with White's son, Leavitt S. White.
2. "Program for a Competition . . . for the Selection of an Architect," April 29, 1911, p. 9.

Chapter IV. The Interim Years: 1911–1922

1. Charles H. Bebb, "The Washington State Capitol," pp. 5–6.
2. Wilder and White, "Capitol Group at Olympia for State of Washington," *The American Architect* 108, no. 2083 (November 24, 1915): 337–44.
3. Ibid., pp. 342, 344.
4. Clark V. Savidge, "Brief Outline of the History of Washington's State Capitol Group," p. 7.
5. Ibid., p. 6.

Chapter V. The Construction Years

1. Interview with the late Noyes Talcott, July 25, 1980.
2. Charles H. Bebb, "Architects Struggled with Materials to Save Beauty of Design," *The Washingtonian, a State Magazine of Progress* 1, no. 3 (March 1928): 38.
3. SCC minutes for August 15, 1921.
4. *Seattle Times*, September 10, 1922.
5. "From Dream to Reality," *The Washingtonian, a State Magazine of Progress* 1, no. 3 (March 1928): 28.
6. Ibid.
7. "Cold Stone," *The Washingtonian, a State Magazine of Progress* 1, no. 3 (March 1928): 19–20.
8. Letter from Wilder and White to SCC, May 22, 1925.
9. *Christian Science Monitor*, September 18, 1925.
10. "The Capitol Dome," *The Washingtonian, a State Magazine of Progress* 1, no. 3 (March 1928): 16.
11. "Cold Stone," pp. 19–20.
12. Letter from Johnston to Wilder and White, September 29, 1926.
13. "The Capitol Dome," p. 16.
14. Copy of contract with Maxfield H. Keck, in Johnston papers.
15. Telegram from Wilder and White to Johnston, February 6, 1927.
16. Letter from Bruce to Bebb and Gould, October 15, 1925.
17. Interview with George A. Munro, son of Alexander Munro and father of Ralph Munro, August 6, 1983.
18. Telegram from Wilder to White, August 4, 1926.
19. Letter from Wilder and White to SCC, April 16, 1926.
20. Letter from SCC to various state photographers, June 11, 1926.
21. Letter from Johnston to Wilder and White, June 12, 1926.
22. Letter from Gould to Wilder, May 7, 1927.

Chapter VI. Wrapping It Up

1. Letter from Wilder to Vermont Marble Company, September 1, 1925.
2. Letter from Hartley to SCC, December 17, 1927.
3. Letter from Seattle Chapter, Sons of the American Revolution, to Hartley, July 9, 1928, in SCC records.
4. Letter from E. L. Gale to A. C. Martin, SCC Secretary, January 25, 1938.
5. Letter from Wilder to Vermont Marble Company, September 1, 1925.
6. Clark V. Savidge, "Brief Outline of the History of Washington's State Capitol Group," p. 13.
7. Letter from Johnston to Savidge, July 23, 1928.

Chapter VII. The Legislative Building's Design Lineage

1. Roth, *McKim, Mead and White, Architects*, p. 155.
2. Ibid., p. 150.
3. Richard Guy Wilson, *McKim, Mead and White, Architects*, p. 168.
4. Ibid., p. 155.
5. Letter from Wilder and White to SCC, April 3, 1923.

6. Ibid.

7. Letter from Wilder and White to Johnston, April 16, 1926.

8. Letter from Grant to Hartley, June 30, 1926.

9. Letter from Wilder and White to SCC, July 1, 1926.

10. Letter from Grant to Hartley, August 31, 1926.

Chapter VIII. The Hartley Imbroglio

1. Norman H. Clark, *Mill Town*, pp. 63–64.

2. Albert Francis Gunns, "Roland Hill Hartley and the Politics of Washington State" (unpublished M.A. thesis, University of Washington, 1963), pp. 90, 189.

3. Unidentified news clipping, Harry K. White papers, December 3 [1926?].

4. Letter from Hastie to Johnston, June 25, 1928.

5. *Seattle Post-Intelligencer*, September 24, 1925.

6. Letter from Wilder and White to SCC, March 2, 1926.

7. Memo from Hartley to Grant, May 12, 1926.

8. Letter from Grant to Hartley, June 30, 1926.

9. Letter from Grant to Hartley, September 24, 1926.

10. Letter from Grant to Hartley, December 30, 1926.

11. Dated sequence drawn from the following sources: SCC minutes for July 8 and 13, 1926; telegrams from Johnston to Wilder and White, July 8, 1926, and from Wilder and White to Johnston, July 9, 1926; letter from Wilder to Wilder and White, August 14, 1926; and telegram from Gunvald Aus Company to Wilder, August 24, 1926.

12. Letter from Johnston to Wilder and White, March 19, 1926.

13. Unidentified news clipping, Harry K. White papers, September 30, 1926.

14. Letter from Wilder to SCC, September 21, 1926.

15. *Seattle Times*, October 6, 1926.

16. "Affairs of State, a Monthly Digest of Doings at Olympia," *The Washingtonian, a State Magazine of Progress* 1, no. 3 (March 1928): 21.

17. *Everett News*, October 26, 1926.

18. *Aberdeen Daily World*, December 4, 1926.

19. *Seattle Times*, June 1, 1927.

20. SCC minutes for July 5, 1927.

21. Gunns, "Roland Hill Hartley and the Politics of Washington State," p. 214.

22. Ibid., pp. 214–15.

23. Letter from Johnston to SCC, September 23, 1927.

24. SCC minutes for September 27, 1927.

25. Letter from Wilder to Johnston, October 18, 1928.

26. Letter from Johnston to Wilder and White, October 26, 1928.

27. Letter from Taylor to Wilder and White, November 8, 1928.

28. Letter [from Bebb?] to Wilder and White, February 20, 1928.

29. Letter from Dunbar to Savidge, December 6, 1927.

30. SCC minutes for December 12, 1927.

31. Richard Oliver, *Bertram Grosvenor Goodhue*, pp. 196, 198.

32. SCC minutes for September 28, 1927.

33. Letter from Johnston to Wilder and White, April 24, 1928.

34. SCC minutes for July 9, 1929.

35. *Daily Olympian*, August 3, 1929.

36. Ibid., August 7, 1929.

Chapter IX. The Years that Followed

1. Henry-Russell Hitchcock and William Seale, *Temples of Democracy: The State Capitols of the USA*, p. 257.

2. "Paul Thiry," p. 17.

3. Walker/McGough/Foltz, Architects, and Lyerla/Peden, Engineers, "Comprehensive Planning Study," April 3, 1970.

4. John Graham and Company and Steinmann/Grayson/ Smylie, "The Master Plan for the Capitol of the State of Washington," August 1982, p. 2.

Detail, bronze doors, north portico

Bibliography

Books, Articles, Pamphlets, and Miscellaneous Unpublished Materials

"Affairs of State, a Monthly Digest of Doings at Olympia." *The Washingtonian, a State Magazine of Progress* 1, no. 3 (March 1928): 21, 48.

"Argument in Favor of Adopting a Group Plan for the Construction of the Capitol Building." Recorder Press of Olympia, undated.

Bacon, Mardges. *Ernest Flagg.* New York: The Architectural History Foundation; Cambridge, Mass.: MIT Press, 1986.

Beardsley, Arthur S. "Early Attempts to Locate the Capital of Washington Territory." *Pacific Northwest Quarterly* 32, no. 3 (July 1941): 239–87.

———. "Later Attempts to Relocate the Capital of Washington." *Pacific Northwest Quarterly* 32, no. 4 (October 1941): 401–47.

Bebb, Charles H. "Architects Struggled with Materials to Save Beauty of Design." *The Washingtonian, a State Magazine of Progress* 1, no. 3 (March 1928): 23, 38.

———. "The Washington State Capitol." Undated manuscript. Northwest Collection, Suzzallo Library, University of Washington, Seattle.

———. Untitled manuscript, June 30, 1917. Northwest Collection, Suzzallo Library, University of Washington, Seattle.

The Brooklyn Museum, *The American Renaissance, 1876–1917.* Brooklyn: Brooklyn Museum, Division of Publications and Marketing Services, 1979.

Bulletin of the Copper and Brass Research Association, no. 43, September 1, 1927. Washington State Archives and Records Center, Olympia.

"The Capitol Dome." *The Washingtonian, a State Magazine of Progress* 1, no. 3 (March 1928): 15–16, 40.

Carlyon, P. H. "From Shack to Palace." *The Washingtonian, a State Magazine of Progress* 1, no. 3 (March 1928): 8–9, 44.

Chewning, J. A. "William Robert Ware at MIT and Columbia." *Journal of Architectural Education* 33, no. 2 (November 1979): 25–29.

Clark, Norman H. *Mill Town.* Seattle and London: University of Washington Press, 1970.

"Cold Stone." *The Washingtonian, a State Magazine of Progress* 1, no. 3 (March 1928): 19–20, 42.

"Extracts from Competition Program, Washington State Capitol, Olympia Washington." *The American Architect* 100, no. 1864 (September 13, 1911): 106, 108.

"From Dream to Reality." *The Washingtonian, a State Magazine of Progress* 1, no. 3 (March 1928): 26–28.

Graham, John and Company and Steinmann/Grayson/Smylie. "The Master Plan for the Capitol of the State of Washington." Seattle, August 1982. Manuscript in author's collection.

Gunns, Albert Francis. "Roland Hill Hartley and the Politics of Washington State." Unpublished M.A. thesis, University of Washington, 1963. Northwest Collection, Suzzallo Library, University of Washington, Seattle.

Hartley's Weekly. A sometime publication, otherwise unidentified, ca. 1926–28.

Historical Highlights: State of Washington. Olympia: Belle Reeves, Secretary of State, Publisher, December 1941.

Hitchcock, Henry-Russell and William Seale. *Temples of Democracy: The State Capitols of the USA.* New York and London: Harcourt Brace Jovanovich, 1976.

Ingram, Henry Balch. "The New State Capitol at Olympia, State of Washington." *Harper's Weekly* 37, no. 1959 (July 7, 1894): 631.

Kidney, Walter C. *The Architecture of Choice: Eclecticism in America, 1880–1930.* New York: George Braziller, 1974.

Moore, Charles. *The Life and Times of Charles Follen McKim*. New York: Da Capo Press, 1970.

Oliver, Richard. *Bertram Grosvernor Goodhue*. New York: The Architectural History Foundation; Cambridge, Mass.: MIT Press, 1983.

Pacific Builder and Engineer 12, no. 16 (October 14, 1911): 215–32.

The Pacific Coast Architect 1, no. 6 (September 1911): 221–56.

Parkinson, John. *Incidents by the Way*. Los Angeles: Press of George Rice & Sons, 1935.

"Paul Thiry." Seattle: Holly Press, 1974.

"Program for a Competition for a Proposed General Architectural Plan for a Series of Buildings to be Erected on Capitol Place and for the Proposed Temple of Justice for the State of Washington at Olympia and Further for the Selection of an Architect." A pamphlet over the signature of M. E. Hay, Governor and Chairman of the State Capitol Commission, April 29, 1911. Northwest Collection, Suzzallo Library, University of Washington, Seattle.

Reksten, Terry. *Rattenbury*. Victoria, B.C.: Sono Nis Press, 1978.

Roth, Leland M. *McKim, Mead & White, Architects*. New York: Harper & Row, 1983.

Sale, Roger. *Seattle Past to Present*. Seattle and London: University of Washington Press, 1976.

Savidge, Clark V. "Brief Outline of the History of Washington's State Capitol Group." Olympia: Jay Thomas, Public Printer, 1927.

———. "Uncle Sam Gave Washington Her Capitol." *The Washingtonian, a State Magazine of Progress* 1, no. 3 (March 1928): 11, 42.

"Second Inaugural Message of Governor Ernest Lister Delivered to the Fifteenth Legislature, January 10, 1917." Olympia: Frank M. Lamborn, Public Printer, 1917.

"Second Message of Governor Ernest Lister to the Fourteenth Legislature, 1915." Olympia: Frank M. Lamborn, Public Printer, 1915.

"Second Message of Governor Louis F. Hart to the State Legislature's Seventeenth Session, 1921." Olympia: Frank M. Lamborn, Public Printer, 1921.

Shields, Mark A. "Capitol Furniture." *The Washingtonian, a State Magiazine of Progress* 1, no. 3 (March 1928): 24–25, 40.

Sleizer, Herman August. "Governor Ernest Lister: Chapters of a Political Career." Unpublished Master of Arts thesis, University of Washington, August 5, 1941. Northwest Collection, Suzzallo Library, University of Washington, Seattle.

State Capitol Commission. *First Biennial Report of the State Capitol Commission of the State of Washington,* December 31, 1894. Olympia: O. C. White, State Printer, 1895.

State Capitol Commission [after 1921, State Capitol Committee]. *Minutes, 1893–1927*. Washington State Archives and Records Center, Olympia.

"Third Message of Governor Louis F. Hart to the State Legislature, Eighteenth Session, 1923." Olympia: Frank M. Lamborn, Public Printer, 1923.

Walker/McGough/Foltz, Architects and Lyerla/Peden, Engineers. "Comprehensive Planning Study." April 3, 1970.

Washington State Chapter, American Institute of Architects. AIA Resolution, January, 1917. Special Collections Division, Suzzallo Library, University of Washington, Seattle.

———. AIA Resolution supporting Bebb's appointment as professional advisor. Special Collections Division, Suzzallo Library, University of Washington, Seattle.

Who's Who in New York City and State, 9th edition. Edited by Winfield Scott Downs. New York: W-W Publishers, 1929.

Wilder and White, Architects. "Capitol Group at Olympia for State of Washington." *The American Architect* 108, no. 2083 (November 24, 1915): 337–44.

Wilson, Richard Guy. *McKim, Mead & White, Architects*. New York: Rizzoli International Publications, Inc., 1983.

Correspondence and Miscellaneous Papers

Bruce, John. Letter to Bebb and Gould, October 15, 1926. State Capitol Committee records, Washington State Archives and Records Center, Olympia.

Dunbar, John. Letter to C. V. Savidge, December 6, 1927. State Capitol Committee records, Washington State Archives and Records Center, Olympia.

Flagg, Ernest. Letter to Governor M. E. Hay, January 18, 1911. State Capitol Committee records, Washington State Archives and Records Center, Olympia.

Gale, E. L. Letter to A. C. Martin, Secretary of the State Capitol Committee, January 25, 1938. State Capitol Committee records, Washington State Archives and Records Center.

Gould, Carl F. Letter to W. R. Wilder, May 27, 1927. Johnston Papers, Archives and Manuscripts Division, University of Washington.

Grant, T. L. Letters to Governor R. H. Hartley, June 30 and August 31, 1926. State Capitol Committee records, Washington State Archives and Records Center, Olympia.

Hastie, John. Letter to Jay Johnston, June 25, 1928. Johnston Papers, Archives and Manuscripts Division, University of Washington, Seattle.

Johnston, Jay. Papers. Archives and Manuscripts Division, University of Washington, Seattle.

Lister, Ernest. Letter to Chairman of House Committee on State Capitol and Grounds, February 23, 1915. State Capitol Committee records, Washington State Archives and Records Center, Olympia.

Olmsted Brothers. Miscellaneous papers in the collection of the Library of Congress (Manuscript Division), Washington, D.C.

Taylor, George E. Letter to Wilder and White, November 8, 1928. Johnston Papers, Archives and Manuscripts Division, University of Washington, Seattle.

Thompson, R. H. Letter to State Capitol Committee, August 22, 1919. State Capitol Committee records, Washington State Archives and Records Center, Olympia.

White, Harry Keith. Miscellaneous papers and records. Archives and Manuscripts Division and Northwest Collection, Suzzallo Library, University of Washington, Seattle.

Wilder, Walter Robb. Letters to Jay Johnston and others, miscellaneous dates. Johnston Papers, Archives and Manuscripts Division, University of Washington, Seattle.

———. Miscellaneous letters to the State Capitol Committee. State Capitol Committee records, Washington State Archives and Records Center, Olympia.

Wilder and White. "Report of Ground Plan," Olympia, August 29, 1911. State Capitol Committee records, Washington State Archives and Records Center, Olympia.

Interviews

Munro, George A. August 6, 1983.
Talcott, G. Noyes. July 25, 1980.
White, Leavitt S. June 19, 1975; September 18–19, 1979; May 11–12, 1981.

Newspapers

Aberdeen Daily World, 1926.
Christian Science Monitor [Boston], 1925.
Daily Olympian, 1929.
Everett News, 1926.
Seattle Post-Intelligencer, 1894, 1915–17, 1925.
Seattle Star, 1918.
Seattle Times, 1911, 1926–27.
Washington Standard [Olympia], 1893–95.

Illustration Credits

Index

Norman J. Johnston is professor emeritus in the College of Architecture and Urban Planning at the University of Washington. He is the author of *Cities in the Round* (University of Washington Press, 1983) and numerous articles on historic and contemporary architecture and urban design. His father, Jay Johnston, was on-site supervisor during construction of the Washington State Capitol.